Passport
to
Mission

Passport to Mission

Second Edition

Edited by Erich W. Baumgartner
Jon L. Dybdahl, Pat Gustin, Bruce C. Moyer
With Cheryl Doss

Institute of World Mission
Andrews University, Berrien Springs, Michigan, USA

Cover and overall design: Margie Mitchell

©April 1999 by Institute of World Mission
Andrews University, Berrien Springs, MI 49104-0220
(616) 471-2522 Fax: (616) 471-6252 E-mail: iwm@andrews.edu

ISBN 0-9671128-0-X

Printed in the United States of America

Contents

Part 4 *Living in a Different Culture*

Part 5 *Sharing Christ in a Different Culture*

Part 6 *How to Be Prepared*

Preface

Mission. Missionaries. What pictures do these words produce in your mind? Thanks to my mom who kept me supplied with a semi-endless stream of mission story books when I was a kid, my mind is flooded with mental images of pith-helmet clad pioneers, courageous women, incredible challenges, and dangers all around. In my mind's eye I see Hudson Taylor walking the byways of China dressed in the flowing robe of a Chinese teacher. I see Adonirum Judson in Burma, David Livingstone in Africa, William Carey in India, and many more. And in more recent times I see J. N. Andrews and his two children leaving for Europe as the first official SDA missionaries, the Westphals, Stahls, and Davises bringing Adventism to Central and South America, the retired seaman, Abram LaRue, blazing the trail to Eastern Asia, and of course, the well-loved "Dr. Rabbit"—Eric B. Hare who labored in Burma.

As SDA Christians entering the twenty-first century, we need to realize we have received an incredible mission heritage. We stand on the shoulders of thousands of men and women who accepted Jesus' challenge to "go into all the world." They heard. They went. And their efforts were blessed.

As we at the Institute of World Mission have worked on the preparation of this revision of Passport to Mission, the training manual especially prepared for short-term missionaries, it has been with the prayer you and others will be better prepared to follow in the footsteps of those missionary giants of the past—building on their successes, and learning from their struggles.

And now as you begin your journey through this course, I pray that God will pour out his Holy Spirit on you and enable you to grasp the reality of what is ahead of you—the joy, the adventure, the challenge.

Go with God!

Pat Gustin, Director
Institute of World Mission

PART

PASSPORT TO MISSION

I

Why You Are Needed

It's Urgent!

As a college student, I remember thinking there were no worlds left to conquer. Richard E. Byrd had explored Antarctica. Hillary Tenzing had scaled Mt. Everest. A few years later man had walked on the moon. There was nothing left to do that had not already been done.

Some people feel that way about mission. All the world has been reached and explored, they say. Whatever is left to do, the local believers can handle anyway. The day of the missionary is gone. There is plenty of work to do at home. There is no need to cross cultural boundaries to do mission.

I was wrong—dead *wrong*! There were plenty of worlds to conquer, I just didn't see them. Those who feel that the day of mission is over are also wrong—dead *wrong*! This chapter will show how far wrong this idea is.

Think about It

- What do you think about mission and missionaries—are they still needed?
- Why do you answer the way you do?
- What facts do you base your answer on?
- Where did you get these "facts"?
- What do you think needs to be done to complete the job of taking the message of Jesus to the whole world?
- Who is yet to be reached?
- What strategy should be used to reach them?
- What are the reasons for your beliefs?

Look at the World

The Church is faced with many challenges in getting the Good News to the whole world. Some of these challenges are in the world *outside* the church and some of them are *inside* the church. Let's start by looking at the state of evangelism among the 13,000 ethno-linguistic peoples of the world. The immensity of the remaining task will quickly become clear.

The World of Non-Christian Believers

There are about four billion non-Christians today who have not been evangelized successfully. These are staggering numbers. About three billion people believe in and practice non-Christian religions. Look at the following chart. It shows the distribution of the main non-Christian blocks. Many of these people can be reached with the gospel only if someone from a different culture makes the effort to reach out to them. Only a minority of non-Christians live near enough to Christians to be influenced by them.

Figure 1: The Non-Christian World
Of the over four billion non-Christians, almost one billion
are not committed to any religion or are declared atheists.
Source: *Operation World* 2001.

The World of Unbelievers

Operation World (2001) lists some 938 million nonreligious or secular people in the world. This group has increased rapidly. It is now 30 times larger than it was in 1900. We rejoice that the collapse of Communism has revealed the bankrupcy of atheism as an ideology and caused a significant turning of Christ.

The Urban World

About 45% of the world's population lives in cities. The remaining 55% are rural, but heavily dependent on the cities. By the year 2025, more than 60% of the world's population will live in cities. In the past most megacities (5 million or more) were in the Western world and had an underlying Christian worldview. Today, most of them are in the Eastern world and are not simply non-Christian, but often anti-Christian. These cities are an "Everest" challenge for Christian believers.

The Hurting World
Tremendous physical needs challenge us:
- 18% survive on an annual income of $100 or less.
- 80 million are supported by garbage.
- 100 million live as street children.
- 450 million are orphans.
- 2.8 million children die every year of vaccine-preventable disease.
- 5 million children under five die of diarrhea.
- 4 million die yearly of tuberculosis.
- 2.6 million die yearly of tobacco related disease.
- 25,000 die *daily* from drinking dirty water.

Source: Barrett, D. B. and Johnson, T. M. (1990). *Our globe and how to reach it*. Birmingham, AL: New Hope.

The 10/40 Window
This part of our globe contains the area from 10 to 40 degrees north of the equator. It spans the area from North Africa through the Middle East and Central Asia to include most of the Asian subcontinent.

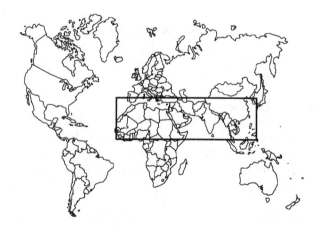

Figure 2: The 10/40 Window
The greatest missionary challenge today! It contains the countries between 10 to 40 degrees north of the equator.

The Least Evangelized World

- 86% of the *people groups* which are less than 2% Christian
- 80% of the world's poorest people
- 34 Muslim countries, 7 Buddhist nations, 2 Hindu countries
- Yet fewer than 10% of all Christian missionaries work here! The 10/40 Window *must be a priority in our mission strategy*!

Source: Barrett and Johnson, *Our Globe*, 1990

These challenges must be met by Christians if we are to be faithful to the command Jesus gave in the Great Commission.

Barriers in the Church

As great as the challenges are *outside* the church, the people of God must also face challenges *inside* the church.

The Uninformed Believer

Many who claim the name of Christ are simply ignorant of the needs that exist in mission. They cling to some half-truths based on a few scattered facts. What many know about mission comes from a few half-listened-to *Mission Spotlight* programs usually focusing on progress rather than challenges. The church must be educated about the needs of mission.

The Distracted Believer

Money, busyness, and the world's everyday cares can distract us from our mission. Debt for an education and worry about the future can hinder our commitment to mission. Criticism of the church and its organization can also cause us to forget what we are really here for. Many don't deny the need for mission, they simply don't get around to doing anything about it.

The Timid Believer

Many of us are merely fearful and timid. We are afraid we don't have anything to share with others. Some are concerned about the response of others to a decision to go on a mission. Others are afraid of change or anything risky.

Who Will Reach the Unreached

What does all this mean? Take a look at the following chart which tries to summarize the magnitude of the missionary task today. It also lists four types of strategies needed to reach the different population groups of the world with the gospel.

God's Missionary Workforce
Figure 3 shows that the world population currently falls roughly into four disproportionate parts:

World D: Bible-believing Christians that take the Great Commission seriously. They represent 1 in 10 people of the world.

World C: Christians in name only. No commitment to world mission. They represent about 2 in 10 people of the world.

World B: Non-Christians who live culturally and geographically near Christian neighbors. They represent about 3 in 10 people of the world.

World A: Non-Christians who can't hear the gospel because they live behind cultural and often geographic barriers. They can only be reached if World D Christians decide to send cross-cultural missionaries. The task to reach them is further complicated by the fact that they live in restricted access areas of the world and often in utter poverty. They represent about 4 in 10 people of the world. Most of them live in the 10/40 Window.

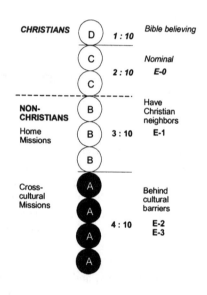

Figure 3: The Unfinished Task.
Based on projections by Ralph Winter, US Center for World Mission in *Mission Frontier Bulletin* 17:5-6 (1995):11.

The Mission Strategy
The chart also indicates four types of evangelistic strategy to reach different people groups:

E-0: Evangelism that brings revival to nominal Christians in a similar culture. It requires evangelistic tools for renewal and revival. Adventists are strong in this category.

E-1: Evangelism to unchurched Christian and non-Christian people in a similar culture. It requires sensitive evangelistic strategies that appeal to unchurched, secularized and non-Christian people. We have had only marginal success in reaching people of this background.

E-2 and E-3: Evangelism across an increasing number of cultural barriers. Progress among World A peoples has been slow. We have done well reaching tribal peoples. We are beginning to be more successful in communicating with people from the great world religions. But we still have a long way to go.

So What about You ... ?

Can you see why ignorance about these facts is so serious? In this chapter we have noted a host of factors within and without the church that underline the urgency of mission today. Any one or a combination of the factors within the church can lead to a paralysis which cuts the nerve of mission. Some have been called by God to fight the challenge of mission within the church and by God's Spirit spark renewal.

There are plenty of mission "Mount Everests" still to climb. Needs are tremendous. Determine to boldly move forward, trusting in Jesus' presence, to meet and conquer these unconquered and unclimbed challenges for God.

Your Turn

1. Which of the challenges mentioned appeals most to you? What religion, area, need, or country is God laying on your heart? What are the reasons for this? What can you do now to work toward meeting that challenge?

2. Study carefully the above charts and facts about the unfinished task. What strikes you most about the figures given there? Do you think most people in your church know these facts?

3. Analyze the people in your "mission field." Where do they fit into the chart? How can they be reached?

It's Possible Today!

The setting is still vivid in my mind. We stood at the view point elevation looking over the beautiful city of Honolulu. Graciously our guide had shown us around the island and it was now the end of the day. We had been together long enough to ask honest questions. "Why," he asked, "are you bothering to go to Thailand? You had a good church job in Northern California. You were near your family. Why throw that away? What is the value of going anyway?"

Most of you have faced that question. If some of your friends and family haven't verbalized it, they have thought it. Certainly you have in your own heart and mind asked it. If you haven't, you need to. In this chapter we want to say emphatically there are lots of good reasons to go. Let's think about them together.

Think about It

- Who has asked you questions about the reasons and value of going on short-term mission?
- What has been said and how have you responded?

The Mission Explosion

The number of short-term missionaries has exploded in the last ten years. Exact numbers for the Protestant church at large are hard to come by. The *Mission Handbook* (MARC, 1998-2000) reports 42,482 short-term missionaries for the 100 largest US mission agencies alone.

The statistics of the *US Mission Handbook* refer to people who went on a mission assignment lasting 2 weeks to one year. Many more went out for ministries lasting more than one year. David Barrett, the world's most renowned mission statistician, indicates the global foreign missionary force of all Christian agencies and denominations is about 425,000 strong in 2001. When you realize that short-termers make up about 50% of the North American mission force, you can begin to see the impact short-term missions are having on the global mission enterprise of the church.

The number of people in short-term missions is so great and the ways they are sent so diverse that numbers are "guesstimates."

The Adventist Mission Explosion

A similar thing has happened in the Adventist church. The numbers of short-termers (one year or less) are exploding. So are the numbers of Adventist agencies sending them.

The largest groups going are student missionaries, Adventist volunteers, and ADRA project workers, but numerous smaller sending agencies and local churches are also getting involved in mission projects. More short-termers go out from North America each year than the total number of regular Adventist missionaries now serving in cross-cultural situations (about 800) in the whole world. Maranatha International alone sends out thousands of volunteers. The South Pacific Division uses some 1000 volunteers on a yearly basis in short-term mission projects. And a few years ago Global Mission began to mobilize tens of thousands of local Global Pioneers in church planting projects.

Biannual GO-conferences focusing on the challenges of world mission began at Andrews University in 1991. Other countries developed their own mission structures: the German G' Camp, GO UK, and mission conferences in Romania, Hungary, the Philippines, Brazil and other countries. These events brought the plight of God's mission to the world to thousands of young people.

To support this exciting trend the General Conference established the Adventist Volunteer Center at the Secretariat.

Why This Trend?

What are the reasons for this tremendous upsurge in short-term missions? Let us consider briefly three of the main reasons.

Reason 1: Travel and communication are faster and cheaper than ever before.

"William Carey, an influential missionary in the 1700's, spent the equivalent of today's US$400,000 to get passage for his family one way to India. That is twenty times the average Christian salary today." (Gibson, 1992:23)

You can see why missionaries in those early days went for long periods of time. Not only was travel expensive, it took weeks and months by ship, train, and even ox cart to arrive. You can now fly from New York to Casa Blanca in six hours and in about 24 hours from anywhere to about anywhere. You can fly most any place round-trip for less than one month of an average worker's salary. E-mail and fax messages can be sent almost instantaneously to most places in the world. The communication revolution is in full swing and the world is "shrinking." In a practical way, for the first time in history, short-term mission makes sense!

Reason 2: Short-termers can give service–yet not disrupt the regular flow of their lives.

Students can give a summer or a school year to mission service and go back to college without problems. Workers can take vacation time or arrange their schedules to take a special leave and then return to their regular work. Retired people are often still vigorous and can leave their home in the care of friends as they serve for a short period.

Reason 3: Churches and mission agencies now encourage short-term missions.

In the light of the above facts, the church is actually promoting short-term missions for the first time. Enthusiastic returnees tell stories in schools, churches, and camp meetings and share their enthusiasm. The increasing number of people who have experienced mission firsthand are also becoming "missionaries" to their friends at home, urging them to experience the same thing.

So What?!

So there is a major movement of people who are getting involved in short-term missions. So there are good reasons for this move. So what? What good do these short-termers do? Aren't these just vacation junkets for people who like to travel? What are the benefits to God's kingdom of all this going and coming?

The church wouldn't be encouraging this if it didn't really believe it was good for the cause of God. Listen to some of the reasons.

Benefit 1: Short-term mission benefits the goer.

You, the one who has chosen to go and serve, will probably benefit more than anyone else! Those who go receive:

- A broadened perspective on the world with all its hurts and needs.
- A chance to test themselves and their ability to serve and adapt.
- Opportunity to make new friends – both among fellow missionaries and those served.
- A sense of satisfaction from the choice to do something for others.
- Realization of the benefits that come from caring for the spiritual and material needs of others.

Benefit 2: Short-term mission benefits the host people.

- They can see the caring and interest of the missionaries.
- They gain new perspectives on their world and the world outside.
- Spiritual and/or material aid is received.

The actual spiritual and material benefits to the host vary greatly. In some cases they are material–in others the greatest gain is probably intangible– a deep sense of the love and caring of those who have come.

Benefit 3: Short-term mission benefits the sender.

- Hands-on faith experience shared in the local church.
- Greater dedication to mission and church.
- Potential for future service at home and abroad greatly increased.
- New vision for what the church can and should do.
- Pool of experienced workers for more short-term/career service.

Beyond all these is the benefit to a global church that is further united through real life friendships that generate international, intercultural understanding and trust. The "communion of the saints" is made real as otherwise distant and unknown brothers and sisters talk together, pray together, eat together, worship together, and dream together—as they understand each other and love one another.

Why Short-Term Mission Is Viable

Research confirms the viability of short-term missions. Short-Term Evangelical Missions (STEM) has done extensive research on the changes that take place in their returned short-term missionaries.

Note the following findings:

"STEM's short-term mission program was found to double participant's prayer and financial giving focused on mission and world evangelization."

"Our study observed the return of one out of three respondents back to the mission field within four years of their short-term."

"A structured short-term mission has tremendous possibilities for increasing involvement back home. Mission-related support activities were found to increase 64%..."

Source: Short-Term Evangelical Missions. *Is Short-Term Mission Really Worth the Time and Money?* STEM Ministries, Inc. P.O. Box 290066 Minneapolis, MN 55429. This report is based on in-depth research on the benefits of STEM's structured short-term program to returned missionaries and their church families.

So How about You?

I hope you feel better about going already! You have some answers for yourself and others. You are part of a growing movement where God is at work. Remember–the benefits of short-term mission increase in magnitude with training and preparation. The STEM research report talks about structured short-term missions that have a good dose of pre-departure training.

That is what this series of chapters is about. Study them as an act of love to God and to those you are going to serve.

1. What are the main reasons for the growth of short-term missions? Do you agree? Can you add some reasons to the ones given in the chapter? Do you think God is behind this movement? Why?

2. Of the benefits stemming from short-term missions what are the most important in your eyes? Can you add others to the list? What are they?

3. Do you think training is important even for short-term missionaries? Why? Give the reasons.

It's a Mandate!

Missionaries are a lot like soldiers. They need to know certain practical things. Soldiers must learn how to march, follow orders, and shoot a gun. Missionaries must learn to practice the nuts and bolts of getting along, communicating, and remaining healthy in another culture.

Something else, however, comes first. Soldiers are worth very little if they don't know why they are soldiers and who they are fighting for. Missionaries are not worth much to God's cause if they don't know who they are working for and why. If those two issues are clearly in mind, all the practical training takes on meaning. This chapter and the next one are designed to do just that. Stay tuned.

- If someone asked you for biblical reasons for going on a mission, what would you say?
- What Bible texts are important to you?
- As a soldier of the cross, why are you going to fight for God?
- What are your reasons?

God, the Missionary God

The first reason for Christ's command to go is that reaching out and blessing all nations has been God's concern all along. God cares. Remember, every person on earth belongs to the family of God—they are His children, and He loves each of them just as much as He loves those of us who know Him well. When God called Abraham many years ago (Gen. 12:1-3) He said that "all peoples on earth will be blessed through you." God chose Abraham (and later Israel) for one specific purpose—to reach all His lost and hurting children everywhere.

For reasons of His own, God has chosen to use *us*. He could use angels or dreams or other supernatural means, but He has chosen to send us to share with the lost members of the family. (Romans 10:11-15). Jesus wants to use us to fulfill His original loving purpose to the world. This is not an option. It is essential. It's a part of being a member of God's big family. In addition, God has linked the second coming to the sharing of the Good News with the other members of the "family" around the world (Matthew 24:14).

The Great Commission

The text that many Christians have quoted to support their mission is Matthew 28:16-20. We call it the Great Commission. This passage answers *seven basic questions* about mission.

> All authority in heaven and on earth has been given to me. Therefore go and make disciples of all nations, baptizing them in the name of the Father and of the Son and of the Holy Spirit, and teaching them to obey everything I have commanded you. And surely I am with you always, to the very end of the age.

Matthew 28:19-20

A careful look at this text tells us the essential things we need to know about Christian mission. This is Christ's last command to His disciples. As you study the seven basic answers, follow the text in your Bible.

1. Who sends?

The risen Christ is the One who sends—*not* primarily the church, the General Conference, our occupation or anyone or anything else. This is what forms our self-identity. Our evaluation of ourselves and our work should depend on recognition of who we are sent by.

2. On what basis are we sent?

The *authority* and *command* of the risen, worshiped Christ is the basis of our mission. Jesus has been given all authority and power, and He commands, not suggests, we go. Along with Matthew 28:19, 20, see the passages in Mark 16:14-16, Luke 24:46-49, John 20-21 and Acts 1:8.

3. Who is sent?
The command is given to all the disciples who heard Jesus. The whole body of believers or the church is sent. The call is to the corporate group, rather than to an individual. Individuals need not wait for a special call, but as members of the body of Christ they are already sent. Rather than waiting for a special call to go, believers should ask if there is a strong valid reason *not* to go.

4. Who are we sent to?
We are sent to *all* nations. The term "nations" does not only refer to countries, but to "peoples" and ethnic groups. The world is seen as people rather than territory or geography. Christianity is a people-to-people movement. Earlier, the disciples had been sent to the lost sheep of the house of Israel, but now they are sent beyond the safe bounds of Judaism.

5. What is to be done?
The task seems to be outlined in four steps.
1. Go. Depart from where you are and cross boundaries.
2. Make disciples. A disciple is a student or learner. A student in the Semitic sense lives with the master and learns, follows, and serves him in all ways.
3. Baptize. Baptism is the vital initiation ceremony and is in the name of the Trinity.
4. Teach to observe all Jesus' commands. Teaching continues after baptism. One of Jesus' key commands is to go share with others. Disciples in turn are to become disciple-makers.

6. What is the source of power for mission?
Jesus promises to be with us always; this is the all-powerful, authoritative, risen Jesus Christ. His presence means that we are never alone. It also means He takes continuing responsibility for the success and progress of the mission.

7. How long does this mission last?
The mission lasts until the end of the age. The mission is not temporary, but lasts until the end of this present age. Only Jesus' second coming and the kingdom of glory bring this phase of mission to its close.

So there we have it–our *marching orders*—the who, what, why and how long of our special mission. It's a very powerful text! Did you ever stop to think about the significance of the fact that this is Jesus' last command to His followers? Parting words are almost always significant—things of special importance and urgency–and these were Jesus' parting words to His disciples. In addition, Jesus repeated it several times (Mark 16:14-16; Luke 24:46-49; John 20:21; Acts 1:8). He obviously wanted to emphasize its importance so no one would forget.

As you know, this passage of scripture is usually referred to as The Great Commission—a command. Sometimes Christians have wished that it was "The Great Suggestion" or "The Great Option," but Jesus' intent was clear: Being involved in His mission to the world is part and parcel of being a Christian.

Now what do we do? What do we have to offer to the peoples in our own countries and around the world? And what does this commission mean for us as Adventists? The next chapter will take a closer look at these questions.

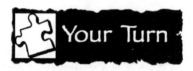

1. Using the ideas given in this chapter, briefly restate how you understand the Great Commission to apply to you. What parts apply and how? Begin with the words, "Jesus said to me, '. . . ,'" and continue for about fifty words. What do you believe He is saying to you through this passage?

2. What other biblical ideas help you understand the mission of the church?

It's Christian!
It's Adventist!

In the last few chapters we've talked about several important aspects of mission, and in the last chapter we studied some of the biblical reasons why we go. We focused on texts that don't just *suggest* that we go, or present going as one of many *options,* but actually *command* that we go. But why is it so important? What do we as Christians have to offer to the world? Many would say that since many people seem to be very happy as they are, we should just leave them alone and not bother them with Christianity. Others would argue that if we don't go and share the Good News of the Gospel with them, they will be lost and it will be our fault.

- Just why *is* it so important for us to *go*?
- Why does Christ command us to go on mission?
- Why do we need Adventist missionaries?

What Christianity Has to Offer

One reason why we "go" is that there are some important aspects of Christianity that people need to know and experience in order to enjoy the abundant life here and now and to be ready to meet Jesus. The Psalmist said, "Taste and see that the Lord is good." In reality, Christianity must be experienced to be truly understood. We will review here some of the basic beliefs Christians share. But we must remember that when we introduce Christianity to non-Christians, we can't just string a list of Bible texts together to "prove" Christianity. They must experience God as a friend rather than just accept a list of beliefs. However, for us it is important to realize that our convictions are firmly anchored in Scripture. Let's review them now.

1. Jesus is the unique source of life and salvation and people need to know about Him.
   - John 3:36: "Whoever believes in the Son of God has eternal life, but whoever rejects the Son will not see life."
   - Acts 4:12: "Salvation is found in no one else, for there is no other name under heaven given to men by which we must be saved."
   - 1 John 5:12: "He who has the Son has life; he who does not have the Son of God does not have life."

2. Jesus is the divine son of God. He does not claim to be just a good teacher (like Mohammed or the Buddha) or a great leader (like Moses or David) or some kind of half-god or lesser god (like Siva).
   - He claims full divinity—equality with God (John 8:58, 59; 10:30-33).
   - His disciples also claimed it fearlessly (Matt. 16:14-16). The proof that they gave for their claims was the resurrection (1 Cor. 15:14-20). If God raised Him, what He said must be true.

Jesus, the Divine Son of God
No other major religion—not Islam, nor Hinduism, nor Buddhism— claims divinity for its founder.

3. Jesus offers a unique salvation—salvation by grace through faith.
   - For it is by grace you have been saved, through faith—and this not from yourselves, it is the gift of God—not by works so that no one can boast. (Eph. 2:8, 9)
No other world religion has such a salvation. They may have high standards, ethical behavior, health laws, a lofty philosophy, or nice people. But they believe that people can save themselves by what they do! The foundation of these non-Christian religions is that salvation comes by works.

4. Jesus offers a universal salvation—all-inclusive and exclusive.
   - For God so loved the world that *whosoever* believes in him will not perish but have everlasting life. (John 3:16)
Christianity is not an ethnic or national religion that belongs to one group of people. The offer of salvation includes everyone in the world! But while

Christianity is freely offered to all, it is also exclusive in that it calls for a commitment that asks one to forsake that which is incompatible with Christian belief in order to become a follower.

The truth is that God wants all people to hear the message—the Good News message that God offers a free salvation based on this unique Jesus. In the Great Commission Jesus makes it clear that we can have a part in sharing this Good News with others.

What Adventism Has to Offer

Now that we've looked at some key aspects of Christianity, we'll consider what the basis is for Adventist mission. Is there anything different and unique about Adventist mission to the world?

As Adventists we have believed from the very early days of our church that we are to reach out "to every nation, kindred, tongue, and people" (Rev. 14:6). That conviction resulted in about 12 million members in over 200 countries at the beginning of the twenty-first century. What is the essence of the message that has driven this mission? What are we to share with the world?

 Think about It

- If someone asked you why you are an Adventist, what would you say?
- What reasons would you give for your belief?
- What Bible texts would you give?
- How would you relate the Adventist message to the unique *Christian* message we just talked about?
- How would you relate the Adventist message to the non-Christian *world religions*?

Remember that some statements and cliches we use to describe ourselves are not understood by those with no Adventist or Christian background. Though most of the individual beliefs of Seventh-day Adventists are shared by some other Christians, the "package" of SDA beliefs is unique among Christian groups. We have summarized them as three convictions that guide what we believe and how we see our mission.

Conviction # 1: Jesus is coming back again a second time—this coming is visible, literal and imminent (soon).

Before Adventism got started most Christians either did not believe in a literal coming or de-emphasized it. Many were post-millennialists. This means they believed that there would be a *millennium* or *thousand years* of peace and prosperity and *then* Jesus would come. What people looked for and labored for was this millennium, not the second coming.

Adventists believe on the basis of their Bible study that the real hope of the world is not a millennium, but the "blessed hope" (Titus 2:13) of Jesus' second coming.

- They read the *promises* of the coming: John 14:1-3: "I will come back and take you to be with me." Revelation 22:7, 12, 20: "I am coming soon." Note the threefold emphatic refrain.
- This coming is clearly *literal*. Acts 1:11: "This *same Jesus* ... will come back in the *same way* ..."
- The coming is portrayed as *visible*. Matthew 24:30: "... they will see the Son of Man coming on the clouds of the sky with power and great glory." Revelation 1:7: "Look, He is coming with the clouds and *every eye* will see Him."
- All signs point to a *near, soon, imminent* coming. Revelation 22:7, 12, 20: Jesus over and over used the word "soon." Matthew 24:4-28, Luke 21:7-28: The signs Jesus Himself gave were being fulfilled around them. The great prophecies of Daniel and Revelation pointed to the nearness of the coming. While this coming is bad news to evil doers, it is wonderful Good News to believers.
- They would see Jesus (John 14:3) and be with Him forever (1 Thes. 4:17).
- The dead will be raised (1 Thes. 4:13-16) and believers will receive immortality (1 Cor. 15:53).
- Tears, mourning, and death will be abolished (Rev. 21:3, 4).

Our Mission Today

Today many Christians who are not Adventists believe in the second coming. This should encourage us to realize the persuasiveness of our position. Many, however, do not believe in Jesus' coming or if they do, it is only in a partial or warped way. They need this Good News of the blessed hope. The biggest challenge we face, however, is the non-Christian world. Millions of animists, Muslims, Hindus, Buddhists and others have never heard of this hope. We must tell them. Jesus wants them to hear about His coming.

Conviction # 2: God calls believers to loving obedience and serious discipleship.

In light of Jesus' coming we need to make serious preparation. Faithful obedience discipleship is important. Adventists have always believed that Jesus is our *Savior*. Nothing we can do will earn our salvation. Only the free grace of Jesus enables us to become forgiven children of God. Our faithful discipleship does not build up merit points which gain favor with God.

Adventists have always emphasized that true faith is manifested in making Jesus also *Lord*. People saved by Jesus should gladly make Him Lord and in gratitude follow Him.

Before Adventism, many sincere Christians saw a conflict between the gospel of Jesus and the law of God. They believed that people saved by Jesus were free of certain standards of law. Some were lax in their discipleship. Adventists believe that both the gospel and God's law are vital and go together harmoniously like the two oars of a boat. The law leads us to Christ and serves as our standard. Jesus releases us from the law's condemnation and His spirit writes the law on our hearts. For this reason Adventists:

- Support the whole Ten Commandments including the neglected Sabbath fourth commandment believing that:
  1. Jesus gave it at creation (Gen. 2:2)
  2. Jesus reiterated it in the Ten Commandments (Ex. 20:8-11)
  3. Jesus reinforced it during His ministry (Mk. 2:27)

- Believe the Sabbath is a powerful symbol of:
  1. God's creating power (Gen. 2:2, Ex. 20:8-11)
  2. Saving grace (Ex. 20:2, Deut. 5:12-15)
  3. The final rest of redemption in heaven (Heb. 4:1-11, esp. 9)

- Accept the Lordship of Christ in all areas of life, including marriage and family, dress, recreation, diet, etc.
  1. Husband, wives, children (Eph. 5:21-6:4).
  2. Whatever is true, noble, right, and pure is good (Phil. 4:8, 9).
  3. Your body is the temple of God (1 Cor. 6:19, 20).
  4. Dress and demeanor are important (1 Tim. 2:8-10).

Our Mission Today

More than ever, in a world where disregard for any standards of morality and decency abound, Christianity should promote a holy life. In a world where hurry and haste lead to high levels of stress, Christians under the lordship of Christ can find joy and rest in the Sabbath. They should demonstrate in their lives both the saviorness and the lordship of Jesus.

Conviction #3: God restores in believers the wholeness of life in Christ.

Christians don't go to heaven as disembodied souls. The second coming restores all of life. Christians should prepare for the second coming as whole people. God wants to restore us as whole people. Salvation involves every part of life and being. Jesus wants us to live full and complete lives. In John 10:10 He says, "I have come that they may have life and have it to the full."

Before Adventism most Christians believed that religion dealt with the soul or spirit of people. At death the soul went to either heaven or hell (or maybe purgatory). The body had little or no meaning. This led to the neglect of health rules and other parts of human existence.

Adventists believed that human beings are a unit. There is not a separate soul which exists by itself. All parts of life affect all other parts. A healthy body and mind help make for a healthy spiritual life and vice versa. Not only is physical health and mental health a part of religion, so are human relationships. The salvation or healing Jesus wants to give affects all parts of us.

For this reason we:
- Promote healthful living including hygiene, abstinence from smoking, alcohol, and drugs, vegetarianism as an ideal, health education, exercise and proper rest.
- Endorse Christian education by our schools and seminars.
- Encourage proper social relationships.
- Oppose war.
- Try to care for the physical, spiritual and mental needs of people in our mission work.
- Believe that when we die we sleep, waiting to be resurrected as a whole person when Jesus comes again.
- Encourage practical, vocational work as a part of education.

Our Mission Today

More than ever a world that is sick, addicted, and living in ignorance needs the message of a Jesus who cares for and ministers to *all* parts of our life. A dying world needs the hope of new life lived to its fullness by God's grace and power.

Does It Make Sense to You?

All of these beliefs point to a fuller presentation of Jesus. I am an Adventist because to me Adventism is the fullest presentation of Jesus that I see.

- A Jesus whom I will see again when He comes.
- A Jesus who is Savior *and* Lord, and who cares enough to guide my life.
- A Jesus who can and does heal not just my soul or spiritual nature, but wants to heal and minister to *all* I am.

The Adventist Message and Lifestyle
Adventism makes more sense to the non-Christian religions of the world than other major Christian groups.

Adventists often feel weird or strange among *other Christians* for things like the Sabbath and our diet and standards. We shouldn't forget that things which make us strange to other Christians are often the things that make sense to millions of non-Christians.

- *Jews* identify with us on the Sabbath and some aspects of diet.
- *Muslims* like our high standards in relationship to recreation, modesty, unclean meats, and alcohol.
- Millions of *Buddhists* and *Hindus* teach vegetarianism as an ideal and agree with our stand on non-combatancy and war.

These people are our real mission field! They need to hear about Christ from people they can readily identify with in other areas.

 Your Turn

1. Do you really believe that Jesus is the unique Son of God who offers a wonderful salvation which is a free gift? Has it made a difference in your life? How? If you really believe it, what should happen? How would it affect your mission?

2. Do you agree with the unique Adventist emphasis presented here? What parts mean the most to you? What parts mean the least? Why? What do you think are the most important parts of the chapter?

3. Do you believe Adventism is a fuller presentation of Jesus? Why? What could you add to this? How has your faith added to your picture of Jesus? Have we as a church always presented our unique message as connected to Jesus? What can we do to improve in this area?

So Why Not!?

Have you ever gone out to eat and not had enough money to cover the bill? Have you taken your car to get fixed at the garage and returned to find the bill twice what you expected it to be? In both cases you were not really ready for what happened because your expectations were wrong. It wasn't much fun, was it? Getting "caught off guard" is never a pleasant experience!

Many problems in the field develop because of similar reasons. Unrealistic goals and expectations along with faulty motives lie behind many of the difficulties that arise in the field. This chapter is an attempt to lead you to honestly confront your goals and motives so that your mission experience can be profitable to you and the people you go to serve. We will also take a look at what it means to be "called."

Goals

One thing that is really important is that we set *realistic* goals. Setting goals that are either too high (false expectations) or too low (no expectations) can cause us a lot of frustration and disappointment down the road.

What are your goals for your mission service? What picture is in your mind? What do you expect to be doing and how do you see yourself being received by the people where you are going? What are your goals? Be honest and be specific! Write down what comes to your mind now.

As you think about setting realistic goals there are several things you can do to help yourself:

• Interview and talk to as many people as possible from the area you are going to serve. This could include former missionaries (regular and volunteer) as well as nationals from that country. If possible you should talk to people who have done the same kind of job you are going to do. What kind of professional goals can you set? Evangelistic goals? Personal enrichment goals? Spiritual growth goals?

• Read and study all the written materials about your host culture that you can get your hands on—especially realistic stories that deal with life and mission in this place.

• Be adaptable. Even those who are the best prepared will find surprises. Expect that your goals may have to be adjusted as time goes on. When that happens, adapt and go on. Realize that adaptability is the most important virtue of all missionaries.

Motives

Now that you've thought a bit about your goals, let's think a bit about your motives. Motives are very important. In fact, they are the driving force behind most of what we do in life. Examining them and dealing with them honestly is a major factor in our self-understanding and preparation for service.

Think about It

So what are your motives? Why do you want to be a missionary? Be sure to consider both your religious and non-religious motives for going as a missionary. Try to list the three most important motives in both of these categories.

Non-Religious Motives	*Religious Motives*

Non-Religious Motives

If we are honest we will admit that all of us have mixed motives. Non-religious motives contribute to the decision to go on a mission. This is not necessarily bad. It is normal human nature.

Non-Religious Motives Many Missionaries Have Had:

- Desire to travel
- Bored—want some adventure
- Need a break from school or work
- Curiosity or desire to experience other cultures
- Desire to learn a language
- Career or job considerations
- Family tradition
- Decision or wish of a parent, friend, or spouse
- Recruited/sold on the idea
- Escape from a difficult situation

Religious Motives

In addition to these non-religious reasons, however, the Bible does give some directly religious motives for mission.

Love for Christ—In 2 Cor. 5:14 Paul says that the love of Christ is what compelled him to go. And when Jesus first set his own disciples apart for service, he first called them to himself (Mark 3:13.) *After* they had come to him, *then* he sent them out on their mission. Coming to Christ first and being filled with his love becomes our greatest motive for going out in service.

The need of people—Matthew 9:37, 38 says that "the harvest is plentiful, but the workers are few." In chapter one we saw that this is still true today because even today, over 2 billion people in the world can only be reached by the gospel if someone is willing to cross cultural boundaries to teach them. At the same time, less than 10% of the Christian workers focus on this group of people without Christ. The song is right, "People need the Lord."

The commands of Jesus—"If you love me, keep my commandments," Jesus said in John 15:15. When we hear this, many of us think first of all of the ten commandments. That's okay, but are those the *only* commandments Jesus could have meant? What about the "commandment" to mission in the Great Commission that we studied in chapter 3? And what about the "great commandment" to love one another? If we truly love our brothers and sisters around the world we will want to share the Good News of salvation with them, won't we?

Mission plays a crucial part in saving people—Our going out really does make a difference in people's lives—"hearing" helps bring people to salvation (Rom. 1:14, 15) as well as giving them a "more abundant life" in the here and now (John 10:10). God sometimes saves people without our help, but his basic plan calls for our cooperation.

Call to Mission

All of this leads us to think about the "call" to mission. Sometimes we hear someone say, "I think God is calling me to mission." Or "*If* God calls me, I'll go." What do we mean by a "call"?

To begin with we must realize that there is a sense in which every Christian is "called." We are called to service, a service that grows out of our love and gratitude for what God has done for us. This love creates in us a desire to share that joy and good news with others. So, there is a sense in which we can say that all Christians are called to be missionaries—not necessarily cross-cultural missionaries, but servants of the Master, nonetheless. But God does call some to a special cross-cultural ministry. We'll look at two different ways in which He calls us.

Some people in history have received a special, miraculous call:

- Samuel, who heard God's voice calling him when he was just a boy,
- Peter and John, who heard Jesus say, "Follow me and I will make you fishers of men."
- Paul, who was stopped by a bright light on the Damascus road and heard Jesus calling him by name to be the apostle to the Gentiles.

Most people, however, never receive a supernatural call like this. Most of us are called by "God's gentle leading." We see God at work in our lives and through various providential leadings we feel God calling us.

- We realize that our gifts or talents especially fit us to serve in cross-cultural environments.
- We realize that our life situation is ideal for cross-cultural ministry (e.g. young, single, strong, healthy, free of entanglements, etc.)
- We receive information (via books, speakers, etc.) that appeals to our mind as well as our heart and "calls" us to serve.

- Past experiences (encounters with missions or missionaries, special times of commitment) call us to a personal commitment.

All of the above factors should be powerful incentives to lead us to mission. First of all, God calls us to Him and then in love, we respond and go where He sends us. He does not command results, but He does expect faithfulness. The results are in His hands, but the willingness to respond to His call in mission is ours.

 Your Turn

1. What are your personal goals and expectations for being a missionary? Make a list and discuss this list with a person you trust with mission or other life experience.

2. What are your motives for getting involved in mission? Make a list and sort them into religious and non-religious. Ask yourself which are your strongest motives? Underline the strongest ones. Are they strong enough to hold up when you will face a crisis?

3. Review how God has led you to sense His call to mission. Are you willing to trust His leadings? Why don't you talk with Him about that in prayer right now.

It's Your Church!

While traveling by plane in Asia my seatmate, who represented a Christian organization, and I began a conversation. After hearing briefly about the worldwide church organization of the Seventh-day Adventists, he stated with obvious envy, "If only we could function as a world church, what strength there would be." This reaction is not uncommon among leaders of other Christian churches and organizations. In this chapter we want to see how the Seventh-day Adventist church is organized to work effectively, how it helps you in your task and how you can contribute to it.

Think about It

What do you know about the worldwide organization of the Adventist church? How can local churches get involved in mission?

A Global Church

When you look at the Adventist church you are immediately struck by the fact that this is a *worldwide* church. Instead of being organized in national churches that are independent of each other, Adventists have chosen to stay in a global fellowship of churches that are bound to each other by a common faith and a strong organizational structure. From a handful of people in 1863, the church has developed into a truly worldwide movement of over ten million people. This amazing growth is supported by a church organization both complex and simple at the same time. The complexity comes from the multifaceted work carried on around the world. It involves some 50,000 churches and over 110,000 Sabbath schools, and thousands of institutions engaged in an incredible diversity of services and ministry.

Institutions

Best known are perhaps Adventist health care facilities, the church's educational work, and the ministry of the Adventist Development and Relief Agency (ADRA). The network of 6000 schools operated around the globe is one of the largest church-operated school systems in the world. Add to that orphanages and nursing homes, over 50 publishing houses, 27 food industries and countless other projects and you have indeed an incredibly complex organization.

Departments

Of course there is also the full spectrum of departmental services. These include Sabbath School, personal ministries, youth, children, stewardship, publishing, health/temperance, family, women's ministries and additional ones as well which provide supporting roles in specialty areas for more successful nurture and outreach.

A Simple Structure

At the same time the Adventist church is structured in a simple way. There are only four organizational layers worldwide:

The local church—A family of Adventist members which have been granted status as a local church.

The conference—A family of local churches which has been granted official status as a conference by a union conference or mission.

The union conference—A family of local conferences or missions which has been granted official status as an Adventist union by the General Conference (GC).

The General Conference—A family of unions which has authority when assembled in session.

The General Conference has its headquarters in Silver Spring, Maryland, and is represented locally through the world divisions.

On June 30, 2000, there were 91 unions, 490 conferences or missions and 47,543 churches organized in 12 divisions. They encompass established work in 204 countries. The divisions and their geographic locations were as follows:

1. African-Indian Ocean Division (AID): Abidjan, Ivory Coast
2. Eastern Africa Division (EAD): Harare, Zimbabwe
3. Euro-Africa Division (EUD): Berne, Switzerland
4. Euro-Asia Division (ESD): Moscow, Russia
5. Inter-American Division (IAD): Miami, Florida
6. North-American Division (NAD): Silver Spring, Maryland
7. Northern-Asia Pacific Division (NSD): Koyang-City, Korea
8. South American Division (SAD): Brasilia, Brazil
9. South Pacific Division (SPD): Wahroonga, Australia
10. Southern Asia Division (SUD): Hosur, India
11. Southern Asia-Pacific Division (SSD): Silang, Philippines
12. Trans-European Division (TED): St. Albans, England

Support for Mission

But what is the value of this organization that guides the work of the Adventist church around the world? There are actually many.

Facing Global Challenges

The first value of an efficient organizational structure is the church's ability to address global challenges. Despite all efforts in the past, the mission of the Adventist church is far from finished. In chapter one we showed that many millions have never heard the name of Christ. Hundreds of people groups are still completely untouched by the Christian message. Hundreds more have not yet been entered with the Adventist message of Christ's soon return. This challenge demands the mobilization of resources that go far beyond local capacities alone.

Strategizing for World Evangelization

In 1990 the Adventist church created a "think tank" to develop and implement the church's efforts to evangelize the thousands of unreached people groups. This initiative, called *Global Mission,* has resulted in the mobilization of thousands of *Global Mission Pioneers* penetrating many new areas and planting of thousands of new churches. In addition, this new vision has influenced churches and organizations at the local levels to take the challenge of unreached population groups in the world seriously and find ways to reach out to them.

Coordinating the World-Wide Enterprise

The General Conference Secretariat is responsible for coordinating the global missionary flow of the church. The members of the Secretariat all have specific responsibilities for calling and sending missionaries and volunteers to specific areas of the world. While the number of career missionaries has not increased during the last few years, the number of short-term missionaries and volunteers has exploded, leading to the establishment of the Adventist Volunteer Center (AVC) at the GC Secretariat which seeks to encourage the further development of opportunities for involvement, for cross-cultural training, and for local church initiatives for worldwide mission. This manual, *Passport to Mission*, is partly sponsored by AVC which uses it together with the *Passport to Mission Video* as a primary training resource.

At the beginning of this new century the church is again establishing voluntary mission service, so common in the pioneer days of the Adventist church, as the defining characteristic of the Seventh-day Adventist lifestyle. The diverse structure of the church has the potential to be a great asset in making this vision a reality again by opening up many opportunities for service and bringing mission back to the local church.

The "Call Book"

Each year the General Conference processes hundreds of calls for volunteers. These are now published on the Web making the information easily accessible (www.volunteers.gc.adventist.org). While many of these calls are for teachers in elementary and secondary schools or English-language schools, a significant number of calls are for nonteaching roles. These are great opportunities for service.

How Does This Help You?

In several ways. First of all, because the Adventist church is a global church you have opportunities to serve as a short-term missionary in many parts of the world. Second, it is good to know that your church is concerned about making volunteer service again part of the "normal" way of Adventist life. This is exciting. Third, the church is committed to supporting its volunteers and missionaries. It provides resources and training. And fourth, it provides different platforms for service. The growing number of opportunities in traditional church organizations and supportive ministries is simply amazing.

Training for Mission (Institute of World Mission)

For a number of years the church has prepared missionary families for cross-cultural service through providing pre-departure mission institutes. These institutes teach future missionaries not only how to live in another culture but also how to be effective missionaries. They have proven to be a great help to missionaries. In 1999 this training was made available to all regular GC missionary appointees. Through *Passport to Mission* the institute's training resources are reaching an even wider circle.

New Opportunities for Mission

One of the great signs of the vitality of Adventist mission is the growing number of mission opportunities available to you. Many colleges today operate student missionary programs. In the United States this program has sponsored and sent out thousands of young adults.

Another indicator of this vitality is the proliferation of "supportive ministries" that train and send out missionaries. Some of them are focusing on pioneer mission work, e.g. Adventist Frontier Missions (AFM) or the 1000 Missionary Movement. Maranatha International sponsors short-term opportunities building schools and churches around the world. Re-Creation Unlimited organizes nature, outdoor and religious activities in state and federal parks in the United States. Outpost Centers, Inc. (OCI) brings together many initiatives providing Christian education, medical care, lifestyle and health education, agricultural and practical training, and disaster relief in over thirty countries. Reach International operates orphanages, schools and youth hostels in countries like India, Burma, Thailand and the Philippines. It is a fascinating list of organizations working with the church to finish the total mission God has given to his church. For details on many of these organizations see the guide to mission opportunities periodically published by the Institute of World Mission.

How You Can Contribute

You understand now how the church is organized to support the worldwide missionary enterprise. You have also seen how all this can help you in your involvement in mission. But the most important question is how *you* can contribute to the fulfillment of the mission of the Adventist church.

At Home

Remember that mission does not start with an airplane ticket to an exotic place, but in the heart of a believer. To be a missionary means to recognize we are Christ's representatives called to witness of His goodness. So you can become involved in mission right now. There are also specific things you can do to contribute while "at home."

At the very least you can get informed about the missionary needs in the world. Start bringing missions back into the program of your local church. Is the mission report interesting? When was the last time the different departments of the church have adopted a mission project? Why not adopt a people group! You may even do that yourself as a personal project. Collect information about unreached people groups, then select one you will start praying and becoming an advocate for. There are some excellent resources that might help you at the end of this chapter. Several other things you can do are found in chapter 26.

In the Field

As volunteer missionaries you will be a part of some aspect of our church organization. It is most important that you go with a positive attitude towards those you are working with. In the remainder of the book we will help you understand why it is so important to go with the attitude of a learner. Remember that if you desire to bring about change or make a contribution to the organization you work with, you need to communicate thoroughly. Always work in close harmony with the chairperson of your board or committee.

You will discover in various cultures and church settings outside the homeland that there are many different styles of leadership and various approaches which differ from the ones which you are accustomed. In many ways the success of your work has much to do with attitudes and relationships.

The church is excited you are interested in serving as a missionary. It needs your support and involvement. As a member of the global church family you will hopefully find your niche where your gifts and interests can make a difference.

1. How do you feel about the worldwide organization of the Adventist church? What do you think are the strengths of an efficient global church structure for mission?

2. Check out the "call book." It contains many current service opportunities. What kind of ministry would you like to serve in?

3. If you are considering becoming a short-term missionary, try to locate former student missionaries and interview them about their experience.

Resources for Further Study

Anthony, M. J. (1994). *The Short-term Missions Boom: A Guide to International and Domestic Involvement*. Grand Rapids, MI: Baker.

Barrett, D. B., & Johnson, T. M. (1990). *Our Globe and How to Reach It: Seeing the World Evangelized by AD 2000 & Beyond: A Manual for the Decade of Evangelization, 1990-2000*. Birmingham, AL: New Hope. A careful fact-filled book which describes the hurts of the world. The facts in the "hurting world" section come from here.

Barrett, D. B. (2000ff). Annual Statistical Table on Global Mission. *International Bulletin of Missionary Research*. This table, updated every January issue, is a great overview of mission and world population facts. For exhaustive datail consult his *World Christian Encyclopedia* (2001).

Bruinsma, R. (1998). *It's Time to Stop Rehearsing What We Believe and Start Looking at What Difference It Makes*. Nampa, ID: Pacific Press. A delightful little book that underlines how our fundamental beliefs impact real life issues.

Bush, L., & Pegues, B. (1999). *The Move of the Holy Spirit in the 10/40 Window*. Seattle, WA: YWAM.

Daily, S. (1993). *Adventism for a New Generation*. Portland, OR: Better Living Publishers. A somewhat controversial statement of Adventist beliefs targeting young people by an experienced college chaplain.

Dybdahl, J., ed. (1999). *Adventist Mission in the Twenty-first Century: The Joys and Challenges of Presenting Jesus to a Diverse World*. Hagerstown, MD: Review and Herald. An outstanding Adventist book on mission with contributions from Adventist missiologists and leaders.

General Conference of Seventh-day Adventists, Ministerial Association (1988). *Seventh-day Adventists Believe: A Biblical Exposition of 27 Fundamental Doctrines*. Hagerstown, MD: Review and Herald. An in-depth explanation of basic Adventist doctrine.

Gibson, T., Hawthorne, S., Krekel R. & Kn Noy, eds. (1992). *Stepping Out: A Guide to Short-Term Missions*. Seattle: YWAM Publishing.

Johnstone, P. (2001). *Operation World*. Cumbria, UK: Paternoster Lifestyle. A gold mine of mission facts which covers all the countries of the world, including Seventh-day Adventists.

Johnstone, P. (1998). *The Church Is Bigger than You Think: Structures and Strategies for the Church in the 21st Century*. Pasadena, CA: William Carey Library.

Knight, G. R. (2000). *A Search for Identity: The Development of Seventh-day Adventist Beliefs.* Hagerstown, MD: Review and Herald.

Rice, R. (1999). *The Reign of God.* Berrien Springs, MI: Andrews University Press. The basic textbook used to teach Adventist beliefs in our colleges, it is Christian theology from an Adventist perspective.

Siewert, J. A., & Welliver, D. (2000). *Mission Handbook, 2001-2003 U.S. and Canadian Christian Ministries Overseas* (18th ed.). Wheaton, IL: Evangelism & Missions Information Services.

Stott, J. R. W. (1999). *Basic Christianity* (2nd ed.). Grand Rapids, MI: Eerdmans. A basic introduction to Christianity.

Winter, R. D., & Hawthorne, S. C., eds. (1999). *Perspectives on the World Christian Movement: A Reader* (3rd ed.). Pasadena, CA: William Carey Library. This reader is a treasure house of information on all aspects of mission. There is even a "Perspectives Study Program" offered in many churches, colleges and universities around the world. For more information e-mail: perspectives@uscwm.org or check the webpage: www.perspectives.org.

PART 2

PASSPORT TO MISSION

Getting Charged up for Mission

Are You Connected?

[The woman at the well] represents the working of a practical faith in Christ. Every true disciple is born into the kingdom of God as a missionary. He [she] who drinks of the living water becomes a fountain of life. (Ellen G. White, *Desire of Ages,* 195)

You are venturing forth as a *missionary*. The main purpose of your mission is to share Jesus, to be an agent of the kingdom of God and to extend the lordship of Jesus. No matter what else you do (build, heal, dig or preach), your identity is to be a *missionary*. This is not so much an activity as it is an identity. It is not *what you do*, but *who you are*. In this chapter we focus on the difference between a nominal (i.e., intellectual, objective, non-participatory) relationship with Jesus, and a dynamic (i.e., experiential, subjective, participatory) relationship with Jesus.

Case Study

The interviewer looked deep into the eyes of the young man he was interviewing. The young man had been born and raised in a conservative Christian home and church, yet, during his college years he had seriously questioned that faith and subsequently cast his lot with an Eastern faith led by a mystic guru.

"What is it that you find in this new faith," he asked, "that is better than the old one?"

The young man paused reflectively and then replied, "Religion is like a can of soup. As a Christian, all we ever did was to read the label on the can, analyzing its contents. In my new faith we open the can and eat the soup."

How Does One Open the "Can"?

As a missionary you will meet people of other religions who have "opened the can." They often practice a religion that is woven into the very fabric of their lives. How do you share Christ with people like this? Why don't you start by thinking about your own experience: When have you gotten past the label and "opened the can to eat"? What are some of the results of this experience?

Here are some practical suggestions to open the "can":
- Interactive Bible study
- Conversational prayer
- Making yourself accountable to a small group
- Dynamic corporate worship with a stress on reflection as well as on the emotional dimension with physical activity
- Personal, practical involvement or participation in local mission or other's felt needs
- Sacrificial giving

Being a disciple of Christ and a missionary requires a deep personal relationship with Jesus that results in a high level of personal commitment and loving obedience. Let's look at these basic two ingredients of discipleship for a moment.

Commitment

Socrates taught that the unexamined life is not worth living. The truth is that it is the uncommitted life that is not worth living. Commitment is the first component in the life of a follower of Christ. What is it?
- Commitment points to the time we made a conscious decision, "Yes, Jesus. I belong to you. Come into my heart and mind, be Lord of my life."
- It is subsequently remade daily, sometimes hourly.
- It involves a continual partnership with the living Lord.
- It is an open-ended commitment, much like marriage, open to a growing, deepening relationship.

If you have made this decision, pause and renew it. If you have not made this decision, now would be a great time to do so.

Obedience

The second component of discipleship is loving obedience to our living Lord. Obedience does not mean perfection, but a relationship.

All true obedience comes from the heart. It was heart work with Christ. And if we consent, He will so identify Himself with our

thoughts and aims, so to blend our hearts and minds into confor-
mity to His will, that when obeying Him we shall be but carrying out
our own impulses. (Ellen G. White, *Desire of Ages*, 668)

Out of this relationship we regularly make daily choices that enhance our
relationship with Jesus. We regularly engage in activities and disciplines
that make these choices natural (e.g., personal devotions, corporate worship, celebrating the Sabbath, giving tithes and offerings).

Commitment Faith

So what does it mean to be a follower of Christ? It means to be a person
who is committed to Jesus and grows in an obedient love relationship with
Him. This relationship we call commitment faith. It is the basis of everything we do.

1. We have talked about living as a committed Christian. What does this
mean for you as a missionary? Reread the Great Commission (Matthew 28:18-
20) and think about how Jesus' authority is demonstrated in your life on a
regular basis? How has Jesus called you to "go"? When and how have you
heard this invitation personally?

2. How do I experience Jesus' continuous presence in my life? What disciplines am I currently using to reinforce my love affair with Jesus?

3. Use the spiritual life rating scale on page 49 to evaluate your present
spiritual condition.

Spiritual Life Rating Scale

Use this spiritual life rating scale to evaluate your present spiritual condition. Circle the appropriate number for each item.

My Relationship with God	1=low high=10
1. I am a Christian and am fully assured of my salvation in Jesus (1 John 1).	1 2 3 4 5 6 7 8 9 10
2. I acknowledge Jesus as Lord in my life through word and deed (Phil. 3:7-14).	1 2 3 4 5 6 7 8 9 10
3. I am experiencing the fullness of the Holy Spirit (Eph. 5:18-20).	1 2 3 4 5 6 7 8 9 10
4. I am guided by the Holy Spirit.	1 2 3 4 5 6 7 8 9 10
5. My convictions about truth and reality are based on the Bible and its teachings.	1 2 3 4 5 6 7 8 9 10
6. I can articulate a biblically-based philosophy of life.	1 2 3 4 5 6 7 8 9 10
7. I am able to integrate faith and life.	1 2 3 4 5 6 7 8 9 10
8. I am experiencing the significance of corporate life and worship.	1 2 3 4 5 6 7 8 9 10
9. I have a regular quiet time with Jesus.	1 2 3 4 5 6 7 8 9 10
10. I have experienced answers to prayer.	1 2 3 4 5 6 7 8 9 10

My Relationship with Others	1=low high=10
1. I conduct myself with maturity and humility towards others (Phil. 2:1-8).	1 2 3 4 5 6 7 8 9 10
2. Witnessing to others is a way of life to me (2 Tim. 4:1-5).	1 2 3 4 5 6 7 8 9 10
3. I know my spiritual gifts and use them to serve the church (Rom.12:1-8).	1 2 3 4 5 6 7 8 9 10
4. I am helping other young Christians in their spiritual growth (2 Tim. 2:1, 2).	1 2 3 4 5 6 7 8 9 10
5. I am helping others with their physical and financial needs (James 2:14-18).	1 2 3 4 5 6 7 8 9 10
6. I demonstrate Christian character (Gal. 5:22f.)	1 2 3 4 5 6 7 8 9 10

Adapted from Jonathan Lewis, ed. *Working Your Way to the Nations.* Pasadena: William Carey Library, 1993, p. 13-14.

Getting to Know Jesus

What I Enjoy Doing

Take out a sheet of paper and make a list of twelve to fifteen things you enjoy doing. Think of different seasons of the year and hours of the day, of group and solo activities. Then do the five steps listed below.

Things I enjoy doing	G	S	P
1. Walking in the woods		X	
2. Inviting some friends over	(X)		
3. Working in the rose garden			X

When you have finished your list draw three vertical columns and mark them G / S / P. Then check (X) the "G" column for those items best done in a group, check the "S" column for those items best done with a significant person, check the "P" column for those items of which you are really proud, and draw a circle around the most important three items in the list. Say to yourself, "That is me. I like me." Behind any facade, this is really you.

What Jesus Enjoyed Doing

Think about the life of Jesus as described in the Gospels and in the book *Desire of Ages*. Make a list of some of the things that Jesus really enjoyed doing and that were important to Him. Then reflect on the questions at the end of the list.

Things Jesus enjoyed doing	G	S	P
1. Talking with the Father		X	
2. Healing people	(X)		
3. Going to weddings	X		

When you have finished your list draw three vertical columns and mark them G / S / P. Then check (X) the "G" column for those items best done in a group, check the "S" column for those items best done with a significant person, check the "P" column for those items of which He was really proud, and draw a circle around the most important three items in the list.

Now compare the lists in worksheet A and B. How many of the items do you have in common with Jesus? Which ones could you do with Him? How many can He share with you? What would sharing these activities have to do with building a relationship with Jesus?

Finally, list three steps you can take now to improve your relationship with Jesus. Maybe you should also put down the dates when you want these steps to be completed.

Could You Use Some Passion?

This handbook deals with many facets of missionary preparation. The most basic qualification for the missionary is *knowing God*. This is *not* the same as knowing about God or even doing the work you believe God sent you to do. Knowing God involves an intimate personal relationship with the living God and his son, Jesus Christ.

The most important thing you can do to prepare for your service is to take the time to seriously think about this relationship. For your own sake and for the sake of your mission, please prayerfully and thoughtfully consider your current walk with God and what you can do to strengthen it.

Think about It

Look at yourself and analyze your spiritual life. Take your own spiritual temperature.

- How much time do you spend in devotional time, e.g. prayer, meditation, Bible study, devotional reading, journaling, etc.?
- Is the time you spend adequate or inadequate?
- Why?
- What would you like to see happen in this area of your life?

Using the simple chart below to trace your spiritual journey through your life with a line showing its ups and downs, highs and lows. Where are you now? What are the reasons for your present condition? Note where your high points are. Why are they where they are?

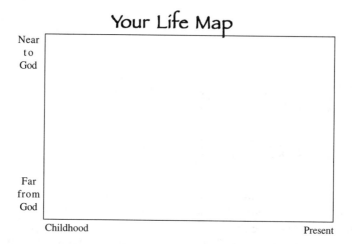

Your Life Map

Near
to
God

Far
from
God

Childhood   Present

Danger Factors in the Spiritual Life
In the pursuit of the spiritual life, we face a number of struggles which fight against our relationship with God.

Struggles

- Busyness, duties, work, school and the stress of modern life tend to squeeze out the spiritual.
- The whole lifestyle in the West—including Christian education—has emphasized the material and scientific rather than the spiritual.
- Many of us have a religion which emphasizes facts, doctrines, and abstract philosophical truth rather than the practice of God's presence and practical issues of relationships.
- Many expect mission service to be a benefit to their spiritual life. In some cases it can be, but in others it can put enormous stress on spirituality.
- Many of us will find that those we go to serve have or appear to have a deeper experience of God than we do. That can be depressing!

Principles to Strengthen the Spiritual Life

What can be done in the face of all this? Certain basic principles exist which, if followed, can begin to renew our spiritual life.

Make the spiritual life a priority.

What is most important in your life? What do you do *first*? Is your spiritual life in that category? If not, why not?

Make a specific time commitment.

Time is the basic stuff of life. What is really a priority for us we make time for. Scheduling to make time for the spiritual life is an act of obedience and commitment. What specific time of day will you commit to God? Choose a time that fits your temperament. Make sure you give God a time when you are awake!

Live and act as if the spiritual realm is real.

Many fail to pray for themselves or others because they are afraid their faith is weak. Others don't share their faith because they are not too sure about their own relationship with God. Faith comes through exercise. The way to grow and build faith is to simply act as if God will do things. Pray for that person who asks for it. Give God a chance to show what He can do.

Be honest about your life and spiritual condition.

Hiding who you are and your relationship with God never works. You can deceive others and maybe yourself for awhile, but you can never deceive God and eventually you and others catch on. God has abundant forgiveness and others understand. We can grow if we are honest.

Be willing to risk and experiment.

I'm not talking about doing something non-Christian! Some people get stuck in the mud in their devotional and religious life. They never pray, study, or worship in new ways. There are hundreds of appropriate ways to communicate with God, but we often get stuck on a few of them.

Share your spiritual life with others.

Many of us are too private and individualistic in our spiritual life. Christian fellowship is important to spiritual health. We benefit if we share our joys and sorrows, our triumphs and defeats, our hopes and dreams with our Christian friends.

Practices to Strengthen the Spiritual Life

Outside of these basic principles there are specific practices that can be of benefit to our spiritual life. These are suggestions. *Don't* try to do them all—especially at once! Try various ones as the Spirit leads you.

Become part of a small group for prayer and/or Bible study.

The need for fellowship and mutual caring and encouragement is met best in small groups. Become a member of one if it is available and if it is not, think about starting one. Many different types of materials are available to get you started including the *Serendipity Bible* which will be mentioned later.

Keep a journal.

A journal is a record of your walk with God and your important experiences. Many people have recently rediscovered the value of journaling and have been helped by it. Especially during your time of mission service you will be helped by keeping a journal of what happens. We all forget more than we realize and a journal can help you later recapture the highlights of your mission experience. God's blessings and answered prayers are easily remembered if they are written down.

Learn new ways to pray.

One of the best ways to enliven your devotional life is to try new ways to pray. If you are entirely satisfied with what you do now that is O.K., but new horizons can be very helpful. Try praying out loud instead of silently or prostrate yourself as people did in Bible times. Use a verse of scripture as your prayer or pray over the phrases of the Lord's Prayer using them as your subject. Try conversational prayer with friends.

Try silence, quietness, and meditation.

Many of us are so used to talking to God that we fail to listen to the still small voice. Try being silent before Him or quietly meditating on a verse of scripture. A reverent listening to God and to our own soul is really a form of prayer.

Try fasting.

In the Bible, prayer is often tied to fasting. Fasting from food is usually meant, but other forms of fasting can be helpful as well. Many of us would benefit by fasting from TV or the radio. Fasting from shopping may benefit others. Fasting for the sake of others is a special form of caring.

Attend worship even if you don't understand the language.

You don't need to understand the spoken language to understand the language of the heart. Listen to the faith and commitment of the people you worship with. Relish the presence of God which comes when people worship together. Don't let your differentness keep you from missing a valuable experience.

Use music and art in your religious life.
If certain types of music speak to your soul, bring tapes or music along. Share the music with others. Music that speaks of our relationship with God is a form of prayer. Use it as part of your devotions. If a certain picture or poster speaks to you powerfully of God, take it along as well.

Give generously to others.
Learning to share what you have (money, clothes, time) with others will change you. Give with a joyous spirit and you will be blessed.

Read your Bible and devotional books in new way.
Read the Bible in a new translation or find a new devotional book. Don't read for speed. It is better to have read one verse thoughtfully and reflectively than two chapters hastily. The Bible is not designed for speed reading. Write a prayer based on a key verse or memorize a verse and internalize it. This practice truly fixes the Bible in the mind and is more valuable than a ritual reading.

What about You?

How you structure your time with God depends partially on your temperament. It is OK to be yourself. You can find out more about your uniqueness through the Myers-Briggs Temperament Inventory (see books by Keirsey and Goldsmith on page 56). Remember that people can eventually tell if you are real or not. People who are genuine before God can be genuine before people as well. A true relationship with God based on time with Him will not only sustain you when the going gets rough, but it will communicate to others as well. That is the essence of being a missionary.

1. How do I experience Jesus' continuous presence in my life? What disciplines am I currently using to reinforce my friendship with Jesus?

2. Which of the suggestions given above do you find helpful for your devotional life? Why? Are there other practices that have been of benefit to you? What are they?

3. What would be a realistic, sustainable devotional life plan and schedule for you? Outline it below and commit yourself to following it.

Resources for Further Study

Augsburger, D. W. (1996). *Helping People Forgive*. Louisville, KY: Westminster John Knox.

Foster, R. J. (1992). *Prayer: Finding the Heart's True Home*. New York: Harper Collins.

Foster, R. J. (1999). *Celebration of Discipline: The Path to Spiritual Growth*. San Francisco, CA: Harper & Row.

Foster, R. J. and J. B. Smith. (1993). *Devotional Classics*. San Francisco, CA: Harper San Francisco.

Goldsmith, M. (1998). *Knowing Me, Knowing God: Exploring Your Spirituality with Myers-Briggs*. Nashville, TN: Abingdon.

Hybels, B. (1998). *Too Busy Not to Pray: Slowing Down to Be with God*. Downers Grove, IL: IVP. With instructions for keeping a prayer journal.

Keirsey, D. and M. Bates. (1984). *Please Understand Me: Character and Temperament Types*. Del Mar, CA: Prometheus Nemesis. The basic introduction to the Myers-Briggs Temperament Inventory. To do a web version of the temperament test go to http://keirsey.com.

MacDonald, Gordon. (1985). *Ordering Your Private World*. Nashville, TN: Thomas Nelson.

Nouwen, Henri. (1972). *The Wounded Healer*. Garden City, N.Y.: Doubleday.

Peterson, E. H. (1987). *Working the Angles: The Shape of Pastoral Integrity*. Grand Rapids, MI: Eerdmans.

Seamands, D. A. (1985). *Healing of Memories*. Wheaton, IL: Victor.

White, E. G. (1964). *The Desire of Ages*. Mountain View, CA: Pacific Press.

White, E. G. (1980). *Steps to Christ*. Washington, DC: Review and Herald.

Yancey, P. (1996). *The Jesus I Never Knew*. Grand Rapids, MI: Zondervan.

PART 3 PASSPORT TO MISSION

Dealing with Cultural Differences

Identify Your Cultural Fingerprints

Most of us remember an experience that made a trip to another country memorable. Often it is some aspect of the new culture we had not yet learned: e.g., greeting our foreign host, perhaps being unable to speak the new language or feeling unsure how to respond properly to the invitation to join the family for dinner. To be an effective missionary we must understand how culture influences everyone of us and learn to be sensitive to the ways of our host culture.

Have you ever gone to a new place where you were not known? Do you remember what it felt like? Do you remember what it felt like when you first met a person from another cultural or ethnic background? Describe your experience?

What Is "Culture?"

What do you think of when you hear the word "culture?" In everyday language we often use the term "culture" to refer to the behavior of the rich and educated elite. They are cultured because they know how to eat with the proper spoon and fork at a banquet, they know how to dress properly, and they listen to classical music. In the context of studying people anthropologists have broadened the term "culture" to refer to the way a society lives and thinks.

A Model of Culture

Culture affects all dimensions of our life. To help us think about the different dimensions of culture we will use a simplified model of three concentric circles that represent increasingly non-conscious and fundamental dimensions of culture.

- *The outer layer:* visible behavior, products, and institutions
- *The deeper layers:* values, beliefs, ideas, and feelings
- *The invisible layer:* worldview

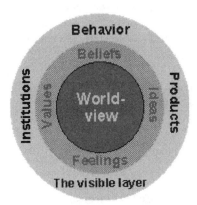

Figure 1: A Multi-Layer Model of Culture.
At their core all cultures are based on a worldview.
Adapted from Kwast (1992).

The Visible Layer: Behavior, Products, and Institutions

What is the first thing we notice in another culture? It is people's *behavior.* People eat, greet each other, sleep, walk, read and work. We may also observe that there are *patterns* of behavior. People greet each other *in a certain way.* All these behavior patterns are learned rather than biologically determined. The products of a people and the institutions of a nation are also part of that outer layer.

Examples:
- In America people shake hands.
- In Mexico and France people embrace.
- In India men may put their hands together and raise them toward their forehead with a slight bow of the head, allowing them to greet many others with a single motion.

The Deeper Layers: Values, Beliefs, Ideas and Feelings

How can these differences in behavior be explained? They are determined by the *values, ideas and beliefs* a society holds about life, the world and people. These ideas could be likened to *inner mental maps* that guide people's behavior and actions. Without understanding these more implicit dimensions of culture, many behaviors remain a mystery to the newcomer.

Examples:
- The Indian way of greeting is important in a society where the touch of an untouchable defiles a high caste person and forces him to take a purification bath.
- Moslems eat only once a day after sundown during the month of religious fasting (*Ramadan*).

The Level of Assumptions: Worldview

At the deepest level cultures provide answers about what is real. These answers help people form their views about the questions of meaning and origin, what causes sickness and death. Cultures are not a random accumulation of ideas, behavior patterns, and values, but systems integrated around fundamental assumptions about reality and life.

Each aspect of culture is inseparably *linked* with other patterns. Even though there are always "loose ends," inconsistencies, and constant change, cultures function holistically.

How We Learn Culture

To summarize we can define culture as *the integrated system of learned behavior patterns, ideas, and products characteristic of a society* (Hiebert). But you may ask, "If worldview and culture have shaped us so fundamentally, how did we learn culture in the first place?"

Most aspects of culture we learn in early childhood before we know how to reason. We learn everyday things like how to greet, how to dress, what, when and how to eat, when to go to bed, how to say "no" politely, and how to relate to strangers, friends, and people in authority. Our concepts of family, friendship, relationships, property, privacy, time, and space are developed through parental training and reinforced through social interaction. Rules of proper behavior are reinforced through sanctions. Additional skills we learn in connection with schooling and career training. All these ideas and skills help us to make sense out of life and solve daily problems. In the end we feel that life is "normal" as long as we can integrate what we learn into our cultural frameworks of understanding.

Three Observations

1. Culture is a total way of life and therefore pervasive.

There is no society without culture. Culture is a people's design for living affecting every aspect of life. It functions like colored glasses through which we filter what we perceive. We don't really notice them until they get dirty, or until we start using other glasses. Moreover, you can't change one aspect of culture without affecting other parts as well.

2. Culture makes life meaningful to its people.

It provides a society's answers to the basic human questions all people face. These answers give meaning to life and provide an integrated logic to those within the culture even though they may seem strange to outsiders.

3. Culture makes communication possible.

People communicate with each other in various ways. Culture creates the symbol systems (e.g., language) people need to communicate with each other in an understandable way. Culture is reflected in language. Thus, without knowing the language of a people it is often impossible to really understand a new culture.

Implications for Missionaries

What we have learned about culture has many implications for Christian service. Here are some to think about.

Cultures resist change—Since culture embraces all aspects of life we need to be aware of the fact that we come to a people who already has a set of answers to their questions and a way of life.

The Gospel is a change agent—Before we can effectively minister in a new culture we must first seek to understand it within its own context. Missionaries have often introduced changes without knowing how cultures change.

Change in one aspect affects the whole—When introducing change we must ask ourselves how this change will affect the total life of the people. Think of a car. You can't tinker with one part (e.g., the carburetor) without affecting the condition of the whole system.

Different is not bad—Each culture operates according to its own innate logic. We must be careful not to condemn people whose customs are not like ours as if they deliberately chose a perverted way of life.

Scratch where it itches—Because no society is perfectly integrated, Christians may find openings for witness in the problems and questions people cannot answer from within their own culture.

1. In this chapter we developed a basic definition and model of culture. When you think of the four levels of culture, what examples from your own cultural background come to your mind?

Behavior

Values

Belief

Worldview

2. Language often reflects the culture and experiences of a people. For example, people living in Michigan are familiar with winter storms and icy street conditions as well as hot summers and ice cream. They use the same word "ice" for frozen streets and ice cream. Eskimos, on the other hand, have many different terms to distinguish between different kinds of ice or frozen conditions. Can you think of other similar examples in your language?

3. Culture is a more or less integrated total design for living in a given society and tends to resist change unless old answers to basic questions are no longer seen as valid. What are some questions in the North American society which you feel are no longer adequately answered and can therefore become bridges to share Christian answers with people?

Conquer Your Cultural Stereotypes

Our culture determines what feels normal, right and real to us, and what we take for granted. When asked why we sit on chairs instead of on the floor we may smile at the inquirer's "ignorance" and answer: "That's the way we live here." We assume that this is the way it *ought to be!* But other cultures have developed other ways to live that may seem strange to outsiders. These cultural differences open the way for cross-cultural misunderstandings, cultural pride and prejudice to develop.

In this chapter we will focus on ways to deal not only with our conscious difficulties to accepting another culture, but also with those cultural barriers that are rooted in our emotions, beliefs and worldview.

Case Study

An American girl cleaned the room while her Thai roommate was having breakfast in the dormitory dining hall. When the roommate returned, she became upset, cried, and left the room. Later it became clear that the American girl had placed the Thai girl's skirt on the pillow portion of the bed. In Thai culture, the head is sacred and putting a piece of clothing associated with a lesser part of the body on a place reserved for the head was one of the worst possible insults. Friends and advisors tried to explain to the Thai girl that the American girl's intentions were only good, but the involuntary reaction was so deep that she refused to room with the American girl again. (From Sikkema and Niyekawa, *Design for Cross-Cultural Living,* Yarmouth, Maine: Intercultural Press, 1987)

Think about It

If you were the American roommate how would you feel at this moment? Have you ever been in a similar situation where you offended someone unintentionally? How did you deal with that situation? Describe some of your feelings and thoughts?

God has made human beings so creative that there is an almost infinite variety of patterns of human living. Each culture has developed its own set of characteristics that gives its society distinctiveness and unity. To learn to appreciate this diversity we must become bicultural. There are frequently some obstacles on the way to this goal .

Ethnocentrism

Most of us have grown up in a one-culture setting, hardly aware of the differences in habits and customs within our own culture. The way *we* do things at home or our group is *normal* to us. People who differ in accent and habits strike us as "strange." When we confront another culture, our normal emotional response is *ethnocentric:* we react to other people's "odd" customs through our own colored glasses. Curiously enough this reaction is a two-way street because *they* also have certain stereotypes of us.

Stereotypes Westerners Have of Non-Westerners

They are:	But also:
Innocent	Interdependent with family
Lazy and corrupt	and society
Inefficient	Living in harmony with
Emotional	life
Slow	Very spiritual
Indifferent	Content
Poor & Uneducated	Servant attitude
Needing help	
Controlled by customs	

Sterotypes Non-Westerners Have of Westerners

Aggressive
Harshly pragmatic
Tense
Discontent
Lonely
Corrupt
Wealthy and materialistic
Dominating
Loud and obnoxious
Competitive
Selfish and self-centered
Attitude of superiority
Preoccupied with efficiency

Educated
Reliable
Strong individuals
Secured better lives
Free of superstition
Confident
Organized

Stereotypes may have their value as quick orientation points to facilitate understanding. But since nobody embodies all the characteristics of a particular list, they soon become barriers to understanding. Missionaries must learn to develop empathy and an appreciation of the host culture and its ways. This approach leads us to remember our common humanity before God.

Cultural Misunderstandings

Another barrier to communication is cultural misunderstanding. When we cross cultural boundaries—especially as tourists—we often assume that the symbols and behaviors we find in another culture mean the same as in our own culture. This is a common mistake. What we have to realize is that behaviors are linked to values, beliefs, and worldview assumptions that may differ dramatically from our own.

For example, in North America it is rather impolite to be more than a few minutes late. After letting your partner wait for more than five to ten minutes you better have some good excuses for being late. Being late thirty minutes is basically unexcusable and rude. But in certain Arab cultures only *servants* are "on time." Those of higher rank arrive some 30 minutes late after the servants have prepared everything for the meeting.

Values and Culture

In all we do we are guided by our values. However, individuals and cultures differ on what they value as most important. Moreover, as Christians we also listen to the Word of God. In order to understand cultural differences we need to distinguish between the different types of values we hold:

- *Personal Values*: These are things or values that reflect our personal preferences and include such things as cleanliness, security, health, and job satisfaction.
- *Cultural Values*: This category includes things that are top priorities in our dominant (home) culture. Individualism, material success, and independence are examples of top cultural values in North-America. Many two-thirds world cultures put more value on community, cultural heritage, and dependence.
- *Biblical (Eternal) Values*: Obviously, this is the most important area of values we live by. It includes mercy, justice, and love.

As you move to another culture you will discover that the most difficult adjustments will be when your values clash with your host culture's values.

Becoming Cross-Culturally Sensitive
If you are unaware of the meaning of cultural expectations you will find yourself quickly frustrated. Learn to be sensitive to cultural clues.

Be a Learner

So how can you avoid cultural blunders and embarrassments to your hosts? Here are a few tips to help you not to judge prematurely from your own cultural perspective as you are becoming a bicultural person.

Become a learner with a servant's heart—It is impossible to become a bicultural person without going through a period of learning. If you want to come close to people, you must approach the new culture as a *learner* and *servant*, not as a *teacher* who *judges* other ways before having learned to understand and appreciate them.

Plunge right in—The key to learning a new culture is the *attitude* we bring to the new situation. Experienced missionaries and anthropologists recommend that we plunge into culture learning right from the start! Venturing into the unknown can be frightening. But soon we see that the risk pays off. People respond with eagerness to help us in our often simple efforts to learn *their* ways.

Don't assume you know—Be aware of the difference between a passive and active understanding of culture. Many mistakenly consider themselves competent in communicating with "foreigners." They may have studied some of the literature, history or art of the host culture, met foreign representatives at school or professional meetings, or traveled to foreign countries. But this feeling is deceptive because it is based on the *passive* understanding of another culture which does not guarantee that a person will be able to interact effectively with persons of other cultures on their own home ground. To become an effective missionary, you need to develop an *active* understanding of culture.

Real Learning—Active understanding of a culture involves not only intellectual and rational, but also emotional aspects. We may accept something rationally, but reject it on an emotional level (like the girl in our case study). Active understanding often comes as we see the limitations of our own cultural background. This is one of the *positive aspects* of culture shock which we will deal with in the next chapter.

So What!?

The goal of becoming a bicultural person is to enable you to identify with your hosts and truly appreciate their culture on three levels.

Reasoning and Rational Thinking (Cognitive Level)—Remember each culture has found its own way of approaching life and its problems. Learn to acknowledge different perceptions of reality and different ways of doing something. There are other ways to build a house than the typical American air-conditioned wood structure. How disease is caused may be explained differently than the typical Western way. Some of these explanations may be rooted in folk sciences and religious beliefs. Some may be more adequate than others. But remember that you are not only dealing with a behavior, a way of doing things or a single belief but with a whole worldview.

Feelings and Tastes (Affective Level)—The fact is that many things are a matter of preference and taste, rather than right or wrong; e.g., how you like certain kinds and combinations of food.

Judging and Decision Making (Evaluative Level)—When you deal with another culture's norms and values, be cautious not to condemn what you cannot understand as an outsider. When evaluating aspects of culture or counseling fellow believers, differentiate between:

- *Good* and worthwhile aspects to be encouraged.
- *Neutral* aspects to be retained.
- Bad or *evil* aspects and practices which must be dealt with and changed.

In most cultures the good and neutral aspects by far outnumber the evil aspects. Thus cultures reflect God's great gift of creativity to humanity.

Rewards

What are the rewards of being a bicultural person? Here are three important considerations to keep in mind when you suffer through the process of becoming a bicultural person.

- *Identification*: As you strive to learn from other cultures you will be challenged to overcome your natural tendency towards ethnocentrism and become more effective in ministry to the people.
- *Enrichment*: Becoming aware of other creative approaches to life that are as valid as your own cultural ways will be enriching.
- *Perspective*: You will better understand your own worldview because you have a unique chance to compare and contrast it with others.

Most missionaries will confirm that becoming a bicultural person may not be easy, but it is worth it.

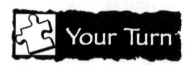

1. Take a look at the list of stereotypes North Americans hold of people of the majority world. Do you hold any of them? Do you think any of them are valid? Why? How might these stereotypes become stumbling blocks for effective cross-cultural ministry?

2. Take a look at the opposite list. Do any of these characteristics apply to you? How do you feel about the way you might be stereotyped by the people of your host culture?

3. As you move to your new ministry, what are some ways you could get involved in the new culture?

4. Think about yourself and your personal and cultural values. What are the top five in each category? How do your personal or cultural values reflect biblical values?

11

Prepare for Culture Shock!

Have you ever loaded a disk that has been formatted for an Apple Macintosh into an IBM computer? Remember the message, "Can't read disk" or something similar? This phenomenon illustrates what people experience who have been enculturated ("formatted") in one cultural setting (our "operating system") and find themselves uncomfortable and disoriented in another cultural environment.

 Think about It

In this chapter we will focus on culture shock—a psychological upset that stems from unfamiliar cues and unmet expectations in a new culture. Can you think of some of the symptoms of culture shock that you already recognize from previous experiences or from your reading?

Why Do We Experience Culture Shock?

Our culture determines what feels normal, right and real to us. When we go into a new culture we are trying to process new experiences through our original cultural system which has not yet learned how to read the new cultural clues. Behaviors have different meanings. Take a basic thing like eating, for example. Besides personal taste, cultural values guide our decisions what, how and when to eat, and with what instruments. To us the new

69

foods we encounter may look, taste and smell strange. In addition there are new customs and often also a new language. Given the many new and unknown factors you are experiencing, it is easy to feel frustrated, out of place and ill equipped to deal even with seemingly simple situations. The resulting condition is *culture shock,* a temporary condition of stress and disorientation a person experiences on the way to becoming bicultural.

Causes

Anthropologists tell us that some of the causes for the experience of culture shock are:

- Inability to communicate
- Changes in routine
- Changes in relationships
- Loss of understanding
- Emotional disorientation
- Disorientation of values

The severity of culture shock depends upon several factors like your personality, the extent of the differences between the cultures, and the way you deal with new situations.

Symptoms

Some of the more common symptoms include the following:

- Irritation over the local way of life
- Homesickness
- Boredom and loneliness
- Overall feeling of dissatisfaction
- Rising stress, distrust, and depression
- Physical illness, especially chronic headaches, hypertension
- Overconcern with one's health

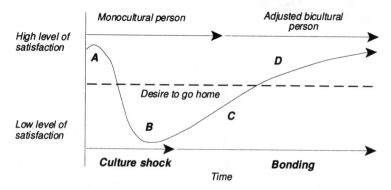

Figure 1: A Model of Culture Shock.
The four phases show that culture shock usually is a process of adapting to stress caused by an unfamiliar cultural environment.

Four Phases

During the process of becoming a bicultural person most people go through four phases.

Initial High (A)—During this phase you usually feel excited, maybe a bit fearful about being in a new country. Your level of satisfaction is high. You are finally there! It's the *honeymoon* phase of your missionary stay.

Frustration (B)—Sooner or later it hits you. You are here to stay. The different tastes and sounds will not go away. Some of these strange things begin to get to you. You can't seem to understand anybody. Misunderstandings seem frequent now. Your patience is wearing thin. The satisfaction level is low. You feel like going home.

Recovery (C)—The good news is that culture shock *is* temporary. Your efforts to make friends are crucial and pay off. You begin to laugh again. Some of "their" strange ways begin to make sense when viewed from *their* viewpoint. Bonding begins to occur.

Acceptance (D)—You begin to feel comfortable again. There is a sense of satisfaction about your work. You are accepting the local climate, food, dress, and customs. You function without anxiety. You make friends and enjoy them. Eventually, you will miss them!

"Danger Zones"

Life in a different culture appears full of potential for cross-cultural misunderstandings and stress. Other "danger zones" are:

- Interpersonal relationships (e.g.: how to relate to co-workers, people in authority, or a seller at the local market)
- Cultural incompatibilities (e.g.: chicken or other animals in the church?)
- Rules of politeness, etiquette and friendship (e.g.: how to say "No" to a request where such a behavior would be seen as very rude)
- Privacy or the lack of it. (That's a hard one for Westerners.)
- Use of time ("Does anyone here wear a watch?) and space
- Communication (Why don't *they* get it?)

Concerns about climate, food, living conditions, and hygiene are often high on the initial anxiety list. These are usually not the most problematic areas of trouble because we *do* eventually adjust to different climates quite readily and we *can* learn to eat new food. The list for *cultural* blunders, however, seems endless. But don't despair. As you bond with the people of your host culture you will become more familiar with the cultural clues. Soon you will develop a new sense of security and belonging.

Practical Tips

Here are a few tips to help you deal more effectively with culture stress.

- Don't deny but recognize culture stress. Those who feel they are immune to it may get it even worse. If you bottle up or act as if you are not affected, you will only isolate yourself.
- Know yourself. Learn to strengthen your emotional security through self-acceptance. God made you special with your gifts and talents.
- Set goals that are realistic.
- Seek a reasonable amount of escape: reading, your favorite music, or a hobby. You may even pack a few books of healthy humor. Humor is often culture specific. A good laugh may help you across some difficult moments. If you plan to stay more than a year, definitely plan a vacation. Ask friends for gift subscriptions to your favorite magazines. In any case, allow time for weekly relaxation and recreation.
- Get to know your host culture. Try to appreciate unfamiliar ways of doing things as other ways to deal with life's problems and joys, even though different from your own.
- Improve communication. Study the language and observe nonverbal forms of communication.
- Don't isolate yourself. Remember that culture stress is only temporary and will pass as you learn to bond with people and appreciate the host culture's ways to cope with life and its challenges.

Record your observations and reflections in your *field journal*. (It is best to start one even before you leave home.) They will provide you with a wealth of insight when you are debriefing with friends, other missionaries and when you return home.

Transition

Transition is an integral part of our life. Some transitions are developmental—a part of normal growth patterns. Some transitions are thrust upon us by circumstance—societal change or personal loss. Other transitions we choose—marriage, education, or career moves. Moving and living internationally intensifies normal transitions and increases the frequency and number of adjustments required. Each of the stages of transition is a normal, and necessary, part of the cross-cultural adjustment process.

Stage 1: Engagement

We have a sense of belonging and security, position and reputation, friends and responsibilities. We are engaged and committed to our lives and community.

Stage 2: Leaving

A sense of disengagement begins, often subconsciously, leading to a re-linquishing of our roles and a loosening of ties. The feelings of withdrawal, exclusion, even rejection can lead to criticism, conflict, and sadness. During this stage reconciliation of relationships needs to occur and proper good-byes said.

Stage 3: Transition

Feelings of chaos, grief, and inner disorientation are at the heart of the transition process. Problems are exaggerated, normal routines disrupted, misunderstandings and ambiguities abound. Grief and self-centered behavior results. Realistic expectations, an understanding of the transition process, and appropriate self-care can ease the frustration and anxiety.

Stage 4: Entering

As we observe and learn about our new culture we make mistakes and feel marginal and vulnerable. Our feelings are easily hurt and ambivalence and fear make even simple actions feel risky. A trustworthy "mentor" can lessen uncertainty and help us begin to feel tentative acceptance.

Stage 5: Re-engagement

Developing a sense of belonging in a new community requires a willingness to reach out to people, an acceptance of differences in people and situations, a commitment to participation and involvement. The support of others who have made cross-cultural transitions is helpful during this time. (Source: David C. Pollock, Interaction.)

1. The process of adaptation is similar to other experiences of change or transition you might have had, e.g. moving to another state, into a different house, changing schools, or losing a friend. Recall a transition experience in your life and describe how you adjusted to it? What were the major challenges you experienced? What helped you to cope with it?

2. How are you preparing yourself for culture shock? List some of the things you plan to do when you will face culture stress. What are a few items you will pack to create your own new sense of "home"?

12

Communicate across Cultural Barriers

"Why is this American so disrespectful when he prays to God? How can he be a spiritual person if he does that?" whispered the distressed-looking woman to her pastor. During prayer the overseas guest preacher, instead of folding his hands, had put one hand to his chin, the other into one of his pockets and played with some loose change. The impact of the message had been severely diminished by an innocent gesture interpreted as irreverence in a culture where God is viewed as a sovereign ruler and prayer is considered an act of approaching a holy God.

Communication is *the* main missionary task. If you are not effective in your communication, your effectiveness is hampered. The basic model of cross-cultural communication in this chapter will help you to be better prepared for the task of sharing the gospel in different cultural settings.

 Think about It

How do you express reverence in your culture? Have you observed how people of other cultures express reverence? Have you ever noticed that one inoffensive behavior in one culture can be quite repulsive in another?

What Do You Mean?

Communication is the sharing of the *same meaning* with another person. When you are in a cross-cultural context, it is at first often difficult to understand the meanings that seem to be taken for granted. Meanings can be attached to any form such as a behavior pattern, a word or product. For example, the behavior of shaking your head can mean approval or disapproval. It is your culture which determines what the different kinds of shaking your head mean. In India people shake their heads approvingly in a way that can be misunderstood by Westerners as disapproval.

Communication is a process of sending and receiving meanings on different levels. They can be identified conceptually to help us understand the complexity of the communication process.

- *Cognitive level:* words and concepts and their explicit meaning
- *Affective level:* the feelings and relationships present in the process
- *Evaluative level:* the largely unconscious critical dimension

In real life these three levels affect the communication process holistically. Thus ineffectiveness in one dimension may impact the total process.

The Cognitive Level

In Western societies this level of communication is clearly of major importance. At this level we communicate words, explicit ideas, and concepts. But other cultures focus more attention on the context of the communication. Anthropologists distinguish therefore between *low context cultures* and *high context cultures*. This distinction may be quite helpful.

- *Low context people* pay attention to words, ideas, and concepts. They may remember the topic of a conversation, but not the names of the people who participated in the discussion. They focus on explicit words rather than on the implicit tone of voice. They enjoy analyzing and comparing ideas. And they prefer a signed contract to a handshake.
- *High context people* pay special attention to the concrete world around them. They notice subtle cues in the physical setting of a conversation which communicate important information: sounds, smells, expressions on people's faces, the body language, and the atmosphere of the room. They tend to remember names and details about events. They welcome your efforts to learn the local language as a sign of friendship.

The Affective Level

People's notions of beauty, style, and aesthetics influence their tastes and relationships. Missionaries must be sensitive to other people's feelings. There is no communication without identification. Even if you use the right words in a foreign language, people still want to feel you identify with them, share their feelings, and empathize with them as persons. In cross-cultural settings over 50% of all communication takes place on this level. You may not be able to speak their language very well. But by attempting to learn it you are communicating that you care about them.

The Evaluative Level

Cultures provide people with standards to make judgments, determining truth and error, likes and dislikes, and right and wrong. We always evaluate what we see, hear, and experience in terms of our own culture. When the messenger does not fit within the established standards, he is often perceived as untrustworthy and the message may be rejected.

Example: Western missionaries are often quick to judge what they perceive to be a lack of morality and values in other cultures. However, it may come as a surprise to them that *they* are judged by their hosts as immoral. Hiebert (1985) reports that people in India considered the dress of missionary women immoral. In their society, the sexiest parts of a woman's body are the calves of her legs. To be dressed properly women wear ankle-length saris. The missionary women wore knee-length skirts.

Form and Meaning

We are often not aware of the meanings behind customs and observable forms that greatly influence the affective and evaluative level of communication. We shake someone's hand to mean hello. In some circumstances it is appropriate to greet a person with a kiss. The custom of *Sirano* men (South America) of greeting by spitting on each other's chest would easily misunderstood in Western settings as an insult.

The association of a specific meaning (e.g., greeting), emotion (e.g., anger), or value with a certain form (e.g., behavior, product, sign) is called a symbol. The fact that people share a common set of symbols makes communication possible. Since these associations are culturally determined, cross-cultural communication is often difficult. Moreover, symbols not only have "plain" but also *connotative* meanings. "Plain" meanings of words are relatively easy to learn. Connotative meanings are often hard to discover and a fertile source of misunderstandings.

- *Plain meanings* point to certain things or events, and not to others of a different domain. "Red" means a certain color and not the color black.
- *Connotative meanings* come from different domains. "Red army," and "to be in the red" no longer refer to the color red, but have political or economic meanings.

So What!?

Culture has important implications for the preaching of the gospel:
- Missionaries need to approach a situation with the receptor in mind. The important element of communication is not simply the message delivered, but the message the receptor hears.

The Communication Process

Here is a simplified model to summarize several of the concepts we have discussed in this chapter.

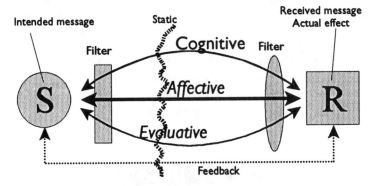

S = *Sender* Initiates communication by sending a message. To send the message he must encode the message and select a form or medium that will allow him to transmit the intended message and that is understood by the receiver.

R = *Receiver* Receives, decodes, interprets and responds to the messages. He is limited to receiving messages in languages and symbol systems with which he is familiar.

Levels of communication The cognitive, affective and evaluative dimensions are present in the communication process in various ways.

Medium The medium is not the message but the symbolic encoding system by which a message is conveyed.

Feedback Response of the receiver fed back to the sender by vari-

ous channels and evaluated for the continuing communication process. The importance of feedback can be demonstrated from the telephone experience. In a telephone conversation we depend on some kind of acknowledgment from the receiver that he is listening, since there is no facial contact which we can interpret.

Static "Noise" factors in the environment which hinder effective communication.

Filters Factors that influence communication on many different levels of the sender and receiver, e.g., current emotional state, personality, education, values, religion, socioeconomic conditions, language factors, culture. Unless we are aware of the cultural system of other people and sensitive to their values, communication is virtually impossible.

Figure 1: Cross-Cultural Communication. A complex process not only on the cognitive level, but especially on the nonverbal levels (affective and evaluative).

People's feelings are influenced by their level of trust in the messenger. If the communicator lacks credibility in the eyes of the receivers, the message is often rejected. If they sense the missionary's sincerity and love, they are more open to the message.

Conversion involves not only changes in knowledge and feelings but the deepest decisions that people make, affecting their relationships and behavior. People evaluate how their decisions will affect their social support systems. If there is no support from social peers, the pressures of their community may be too great.

Moreover, symbols also reflect the worldview of people, the *implicit* and hidden assumptions they make about reality. Words for "God," "good," "evil," "salvation," and "sin" often have *hidden* meanings that are hard to discover because they are taken for granted and not talked about.

1. *Images of Mission* (Hagerstown, MD: Review and Herald, 1995) is an impressive pictorial record of the diversity of the Seventh-day Adventist church around the world. Pictures often reflect the cultural origin of the missionary who took them. On page 19 in *Images* you will find a photo showing a poster advertizing a Revelation Seminar in Shanghai, China. A lonely man in front of a monumental stone wall (the Ten Commandments) in a judgment hall full of angels dressed in white. How do you think Chinese persons feel about such a painting of the last judgment? You may want to find out if you can. How would you paint this picture differently to communicate culturally sensitive meaning?

2. In North America sexual immorality is seen as an enormous sin. Missionaries from that part of the world tend to stress proper sexual behavior. In South Asia, however, a cardinal sin is to lose one's temper. Too often Western missionaries are completely unaware of the implications of impatient behavior on the communication process (especially with their servants). How do you feel about this? Do you have a problem in this area? What will you do about it?

3. Take a look at the model of communication presented in this chapter. Do you agree with it? How would you modify it? How will you use it to become a more effective communicator?

13

Deal with Conflicts

One of the most common experiences in cross-cultural service is conflict. Even when working or traveling with people you know well, misunderstandings happen and can develop into full-fledged conflicts. Add to that cultural differences and the potential for conflict is even greater. Missionaries need to understand the nature of conflict and appropriate ways to deal with it.

Think about It

What are some of the ways people react to conflict? How do you feel yourself when you are in a conflict situation? How do you tend to react to conflict?

What Is Conflict?

Conflict is the common human experience of managing differences. People disagree or differ in many ways: roles and behaviors, beliefs and expectations, worldview, attitudes and values. How we tend to react in conflict is partly determined by our personalities. Beyond that, a missionary must be aware of the fact that every people has its own—often unwritten—rules to handle disputes and differences in a culturally appropriate way.

Not all conflicts have the same intensity. There are probably at least four stages or levels of conflict. Can you think of some examples?

- Level 1: Unrest
- Level 2: Disagreement
- Level 3: Confrontation
- Level 4: Outright Conflict

How We Deal with Conflict

Each one of us has developed a pattern of behavior in interpersonal conflict that reflects our past experiences, our personality and our "theology of conflict." These patterns can become so predictable that experts call them *styles* of conflict management.

Some of these styles are more appropriate in one situation than in another. By understanding your own preferred pattern and how each style tends to impact a situation, you can learn to make more conscious and productive choices.

Five typical styles of dealing with conflict have been listed by Norman Shawchuck in *How to Manage Conflict in the Church* (Schaumburg, IL: Spiritual Growth Resources, 1983). Here is a brief summary.

---

1 Avoiding (The Passive Turtle)

Motto:
"I will stay out of it."

Biblical Example:
Adam avoiding God after sinning (Gen. 3:9-10)

Intent:
- To stay out of conflict.
- Be neutral.
- Others are responsible for the conflict.
- "Not my problem."
- "I don't care."
- Sometimes: Conflict-is-wrong attitude.

Behavior:
- Unassertive and passive.
- Does not cooperate in defining the conflict.
- Often denial that problem exists.
- Withdrawal.

Result:
- I lose—you lose.
- Negative nonproductive strategy.
- Abdicating responsibility.
- Produces frustration.

When Appropriate:
- When problems not your responsibility or without long-term importance.
- Participants too fragile and insecure.
- When differences are irreconcilable.
- Confrontation will not accomplish anything.
- Some parents should use this style.

Don't Use:
- For important issues.
- When issues will not disappear but continue to build.

---

2 Accommodating (Lovable Teddy Bear)

Motto:
"I will give in."

Biblical Example:
Lot and Abraham (Gen 13:5-9)

Intent:
- To preserve relationships at any cost.
- Getting along seen as more important than the conflict issues.
- Relationships more important than work and goals.

Action:
- To preserve relationships at any cost.
- Assertive regarding the solutions of others but not his own.
- May even be willing to accept the blame for the conflict.

Results:
- I lose—you win.
- Does not resolve conflict.
- Winners assume their ways are superior.
- Unrealistic.
- Ends up a doormat.

When Appropriate:
- Relatively minor issues
- When one's own ideas are not helpful and better or several equally good solutions are offered.
- When long-term relationships are more important than the short-range conflicts.

Don't Use:
- To evade issue.
- When others are willing to deal with the issue.

3 Compromising (The Wily Fox)

Motto:
"I meet you halfway."

Biblical Example:
Council in Jerusalem (Acts 15:1-35)

Intent:
- Win a little— lose a little.
- To partially satisfy all parties.
- Popular with politicians, collective bargainers, and international negotiators.

Action:
- Negotiation and bargaining.
- We agree to x if you agree to y.
- Flexible style.
- Uses persuasion if not manipulation.

Results:
- Both win some and lose some.
- May result in ineffective solutions.
- Does not engender full commitments to carry solutions out.
- May salvage stalemates.
- Often achieves the good since the best is not possible.

When Appropriate:
- When goals of all parties are valid.
- Differences are not worth fighting for.
- Time doesn't allow for deeper solutions.

Don't Use:
- To accommodate unrealistic positions or bad solutions.
- If commitment is doubted.

4 Competing (The Aggressive Shark)

Motto:
"I will get my way."

Biblical Example:
Saul's anger toward Jonathan (2 Sam. 20:30-33)

Intent:
• To win.
• Assumes that there are only two possibilities in conflict: to win and to lose.
• Winning is better.
• His own values, goals, ideas are of supreme importance.

Action:
• Assertiveness, domination if necessary.
• Smooth diplomacy to raw power, but with the same goal: to win.
• May manipulate.
• Message: I know what is best.

Results:
• I win - you lose.
• Creates polarization.
• Frustrates the defeated.
• Often grows hostile.
• Does not work: you may win the battle but not the war.

When Appropriate:
• Decision must be made very quickly.
• For necessary but unpopular decision.
• A person's future depends on it.

Don't Use:
• Destroying others to get one's way.
• Loser can't express needs.

5 Collaborating (The Wise Owl)

Motto:
"Let's work together for everyone's good.

Biblical Example:
Wisdom of open communication (Prov. 27:5-6) Not often practiced.

Intent:
• To achieve a win-win for all parties.
• Issues *and* people are considered important.
• Assumes people are able to solve their own problems.
• Appreciates the value of each person.
• Respects each party's ideas and goals, while also seeking to maintain a good relationships.

Action:
• Assertive, also flexible.
• Commitment to win-win solutions.
• Promotes respect, open communication.
• Firm yet sensitive to people's feelings.
• Ensures fairness.
• All parties must be willing to cooperate.

Results.
• I win—you win.
• Creates participation.
• Honest clarification of issues/interests.
• Shared decision-making and implementation.
• Creativity mobilized.
• You get what you want in an often new way.

When Appropriate:
• In most conflicts.
• Esp. Involving long-term goals and relationships.
• Requires maturity and patience.
• Should be practiced more often.

Don't Use:
• When conditions and time are too short.
• When commitments are not present.
• When abilities are not present.

Cultural Differences

Each one of us has a preferred personal conflict management style. But in cross-cultural situations we must also be aware how your host culture approaches conflict management. To know what is appropriate in a given situation be sensitive to at least these three questions:

1. How is conflict dealt with in my host culture?
2. How is conflict handled in my own culture?
3. What are the biblical principles that can be used to interact with cultural traditions redemptively?

Some factors that influence the way societies handle conflicts are:

- *Social organization*: Who has authority? What are the social roles of those involved? How are decisions made?
- *Power distance:* How much power does a leader have in comparison with other people?
- *Individualism*: How much freedom do individuals have to make their own decisions?
- *Group orientation:* How important is the group?
- *Channels*: Are there appropriate "channels" to resolve conflicts?

How do these factors influence the way conflict, both group or personal, is handled? In the individualistic society in North America we allow open criticism and face-to-face confrontation as ways to resolution. We also use committees to balance individual freedom. In group-oriented Asian cultures, where "saving face" is an important concern, it may be unacceptable to expose the vulnerability of individuals. Conflicts may be resolved through mediators. Other societies settle conflicts and make decisions by consensus announced only after lengthy periods of informal discussion and consideration. Committees may not work effectively in such contexts.

So What!?

Western missionaries are often unaware of their own cultural context in which they have learned how to deal with conflict. Moreover, Christians fail to appreciate that the Bible has been written to people in specific social contexts applying universal kingdom principles for specific social action. The result is that Western missionaries often choose biblical passages in harmony with the values of *their own* social environments and apply them in ways which may violate other fundamental biblical values, such as humility, love, and respect for one another. How we use Matthew 18 is a case in point.

Biblical Principles

In Matthew 18:15-17 Jesus instructed his disciples how to deal with sin in the church. How do we approach this text in our Western culture?

- *Private confrontation*: We often understand Jesus' instruction as a command for open, private, face to face confrontation.
- *Public confrontation*: If this procedure is not successful the next step is to follow it up by an authority rule strategy leading to public final confrontation.

While there may be times for public confrontation of sin in any culture, the process described reflects an interpretation of scripture that is derived from Western roots. Those who have lived in a group-oriented culture know how inadequate and destructive such an approach can be. But what are the alternatives? When you take a look at the whole chapter as the context for this passage (esp. verses 4, 14, 19, 23, and 35) you find that Jesus is stressing qualities like humility, sensitivity, compassion, unity, servanthood, and a forgiving spirit. This is important as you think about applying Christ's instruction in non-confrontation-oriented cultures.

Instead of using Matthew 18:15-17 as a call for confrontation procedures unacceptable in cultures that value group relationships, try to use the powerful base principles that this text contains. Do not confuse procedure with principle and form with meaning. Furthermore make sure you also consider other scriptural instruction on how to deal with conflict.

Be Sensitive

The scope of conflict—Exercise caution and wisdom in situations of conflict by restricting the scope of the disagreement to "just between the two of you." Remember the proverbs that instruct people to exercise caution (Prov. 3:30; 20:3; 25:8).

The goal of conflict resolution—Restore relationships with those with whom you have disagreements. Jesus affirms the centrality of love in neighborly relationships (Matth. 22:39 cf. Phil. 2:3).

Use the counsel of others—Humbly rely on the counsel of others, rather than on personal judgment. The purpose of having two or three witnesses is to invite counsel as well as support. James 1:19 admonishes to be "slow to anger" and Paul encourages us to patience and unity (Eph. 4:2-3), and to avoid strife (2 Tim. 2:14; 1 Cor. 3:3).

The use of mediators—The Bible contains valuable examples of the use of mediators, messengers, gifts, feasts of peace for restoring peace. See 2 Samuel 3 (Abner and David), 1 Samuel 25 (Abigail, Nabal and David), 1 and 2 Samuel (Jonathan and Saul).

Implications for Missionaries

As a missionary, you will be more effective when you seek to apply biblical principles in a cross-culturally sensitive way. The following principles might help you in this endeavor.

1. Understand the social context in which you practice ministry to determine whether direct or indirect modes of decision making and confrontation are appropriate.

2. When you have understood your environment, examine how you can live a transformed life, employing kingdom principles to engage the people of that society to redemptively deal with conflict and discover the bond of unity and peace.

3. Understand that the social environment of the Book of Acts and the Epistles is characterized by formal confrontation, majority rule, and arbitration of disputes. Distinguish between process and ethical/moral principle. People are saved not through procedures but through a right relationship with Christ and the transformation that comes through Him.

As you grow more sensitive to cross-cultural factors you will also become more effective in dealing with conflict.

1. Review the five styles of handling conflict. Which styles have you used? In what situations? How effective are you in resolving conflicts without creating bitterness in your own culture?

2. Review the ways the principles of Matthew 18 are employed in the resolution of conflict in your own culture. How do you feel about these? Can conflict be approached the same way in your host culture? Why don't you try to discuss this question with someone who knows your host culture well. Then jot down the most important principles you learned.

3. How do you feel about the key principles for cross-cultural conflict management we discussed in this chapter? Write in your own words how you will use these principles in your ministry to be an agent of peace and unity.

Resources for Further Study

Brewster, E. T., & Brewster, E. S. (1999). The Difference Bonding Makes. In R. D. Winter & S. C. Hawthorne, eds. *Perspectives on the World Christian Movement: A Reader* (3rd ed., pp. 444-448). Pasadena, CA: William Carey Library.

Donovan, K. (1991). *Growing through Stress*. Sydney, Australia: Aquila Press.

Elmer, D. (1993). *Cross-cultural Conflict: Building Relationships for Effective Ministry*. Downer's Grove, IL: IVP.

Hesselgrave, D. J. (1999). The Role of Culture in Communication. In R. D. Winter & S. C. Hawthorne, eds. *Perspectives* (3rd ed., pp. 392-396).

Hiebert, P. G. (1985). *Anthropological Insights for Missionaries*. Grand Rapids: Baker.

Hiebert, P. G. (1999). Cultural Differences and the Communication of the Gospel. In R. D. Winter & S. C. Hawthorne, eds. *Perspectives* (3rd ed., pp. 373-383).

Larson, D. N. (1999). The Viable Missionary: Learner, Trader, Story Teller. In R. D. Winter & S. C. Hawthorne, eds. *Perspectives* (3rd ed., pp. 438-443).

Lingenfelter, S. (1998). *Transforming Culture: A Challenge for Christian Mission* (2nd ed.). Grand Rapids, MI: Baker.

Nussbaum, S. (1998). *The ABCs of American Culture: Understanding the American People through Their Common Sayings*. Colorado Springs, CO: Global Mapping International.

Nwanna, G. I. (1998). *Do's and Don'ts Around the World: A Country Guide to Cultural and Social Taboos and etiquette*. The series includes volumes on Africa, the Caribbean, Europe, the Middle East, Oceania and Japan, and Russia. Baltimore, MD: World Travel Institute.

Palmer, D. C. (1990). *Managing Conflict Creatively: A Guide for Missionaries and Christian Workers*. Pasadena, CA: William Carey Library.

Reyburn, W. D. (1999). Identification in the Missionary Task. In R. D. Winter & S. C. Hawthorne, eds. *Perspectives* (pp. 449-455).

Richardson, D. (1999). Redemptive Analogy. In R. D. Winter & S. C. Hawthorne, eds. *Perspectives* (3rd ed., pp. 397-403).

PART PASSPORT TO MISSION

4

Living in a Different Culture

The Incarnational Missionary

So, you've made the decision. You're definitely going to be a missionary. Now what? You have a jillion questions, right? And several thousand concerns (not to mention several thousand more that your mother has). You're excited, of course, but... You're committed, but what if... It seems like a great idea, but what about....? Is that how you're feeling right now?

Well, join the club. We've all had questions and doubts and concerns (sometimes called fears). Let's face it—we're going into unknown territory. A new place. New job. New culture. New language. New challenges. We want to succeed. We want to make a difference. We want to be "good missionaries". But how do we go about it? And in addition most of us have heard "horror stories" about western missionaries (Americans or Europeans) who have gone abroad and been really obnoxious—the "Ugly American" syndrome. And we definitely don't want to do that—right?

How can we avoid coming across as arrogant and culturally insensitive? How can we live in a new place in such a way that we do not offend, repel, antagonize and in other ways alienate those whom we are trying to reach? In other words, how can we be successful missionaries who draw people *to* ourselves, Jesus and the gospel, rather than turning them *away*?

How God Modeled Incarnational Mission

Let's begin our search for some clues on "how to be a successful mission-ary" by looking at some significant portraits of God and Jesus (our model missionaries) that are scattered throughout the Bible. From these "snap-shots" we can see how they interacted with people who were different, even estranged from them. Then we can ask what their example means to us.

God with Us

At the very beginning of recorded history, before sin even entered, we find an important picture of God. He is walking and talking with Adam and Eve in the Garden of Eden at the close of each day. There they are. Together. Simple though it is, this scenario sets the stage for the thousands of years of interaction between God and humanity that have followed. God has always wanted to be together with his people.

Then when God brought the children of Israel out of Egypt and He wanted to show them clearly that He was there with them still, He stayed right in their midst in the form of a pillar of cloud by day and fire by night. And when He gave them the directions for the building of the tabernacle (and later the temple) He clearly stated that it was for the purpose of living "among them." Together, again.

Last of all we see Jesus, referred to as "Emmanuel" in both Isaiah and Matthew: "God with us." God left behind the glories of heaven, the compan-ionship of angel friends, the food, clothes, language, and culture of heaven, to come to this backward, dirty, degenerate mission field called earth to be *with* His people again. He lived with them for 30 years—eating their food, wearing their clothes, speaking their language, thinking their thoughts. To-gether again.

This is what we call "the incarnation." And this is God's example to us of what real mission is about. It's being *with* the people we've come to serve. Close. Together. Living as much like them as is possible. We sometimes refer to this as "missionary identification."

How Jesus Identified with Us

What did incarnation mean for Jesus? In 2 Corinthians 8:9 we read, "For you know the grace of our Lord Jesus Christ, that though He was rich, yet for your sakes He became poor, so that you through His poverty might become rich." Just exactly what this meant is outlined very clearly in Philippians 2. First of all He gave up His *status*—equality with God and His identity as God. (He still was God, of course, but He did not use His divinity or was not recognizable as God.) In addition, He gave up His *independence* and actually became a servant.

He also gave up His *immunity* to the vicissitudes of life and became weak and vulnerable. Lastly, He *totally identified* with the people He came to serve and save. Jesus was a first century Jew living in a tiny underdeveloped country in the Middle East.

The incarnation of Christ helps us to understand something very practical. By following the example of Christ in identifying with people we are in fact saying to the people we are serving:
- Your ways are good and valuable and I respect them.
- I am not superior or better than you.
- I like you and want to understand you better.
- I want to learn from you.
But what does that mean to us today in the nitty-gritty, everyday areas of life?

Attitudes of an Incarnational Missionary

The first (and most important) thing that is affected is our attitude.
- We consider others as our equals, even superiors, accepting the role of a learner.
- We also become a servant, giving up our rights to be "in charge."
- We cast in our lot with those around us, experiencing life as they do, as much as possible.
- We try to see the world through their eyes, rather than asking them to look through ours.
- We choose to see the good around us, cultivating a sense of tolerance and ultimate acceptance.
- We admit that our own culture is less than perfect. We remember that

   ...[t]here is no person, no nation, that is perfect in every habit and thought. One must learn of another. Therefore God wants the different nationalities to mingle together, to be one in judgement, one in purpose. Then the union that there is in Christ will be exemplified. (Ellen White, *Historical Sketches of SDA Missions,* 136.)

Behaviors of an Incarnational Missionary

Secondly, incarnation or identification affects the way we live from day to day—eating, dressing, housing, shopping, playing, and even worshiping. Though we may never be able to do everything in the same way as those of our host culture do, we nevertheless need to make an effort to adapt to as many ways as we can.

Eating

Whether the staple food is rice, noodles, pasta, potatoes, or corn meal mush, we learn to eat it gracefully, hopefully even with gusto. We curb our urge to spend most of our salary on imported Western foods that others can only see as an unnecessary luxury—a silent symbol of our separateness.

Dressing

Whenever possible, we try to fit in with whatever the appropriate dress is for the place and position we have been asked to fill. How do teachers (nurses/pastors/government agents) dress? What is considered modest/immodest? What is considered ostentatious? What is considered inappropriate for church? work? the beach? In other words, how can you dress in such a way that you will blend in the best and not cause offense? What that means is that if women go swimming in dresses instead of swimming suits and don't wear shorts even for sporting events in the place you are serving, you will want to tuck those items of clothing in the bottom of your drawer and leave them there for your entire stay, just as Jesus tucked his robes of glory away and never donned them during his entire 30 years on earth—not even for festive occasions. And if men do not wear beards or neckties or bright-colored shirts in the place you are serving, you will follow Jesus' example by getting rid of yours for the duration of your term of service.

Housing

In times past, it was quite customary for Westerners, including missionaries, to live in very nice houses—much nicer that most of the local people could ever afford. As you can imagine, this caused a great deal of real ill-will. Fortunately, in many places this is no longer true, though to some extent the tendency has survived. There is, however, still a tendency for us to take our standards of living with us, perhaps subconsciously expecting things to be "just like back home"—tiled bathrooms and kitchens, hot water heaters, spacious rooms, etc. As incarnational missionaries we will be willing to accept housing that is much simpler and plainer than we would have back home. If single teachers live in a room with a small bathroom attached, and the only furniture is a bed, wardrobe, table and two stools, we will accept that housing with grace.

Shopping

Most places we serve have a variety of options for shopping. There will probably be local markets, small shops, and in many cases, various types of department stores—ranging from relatively modestly-priced ones that many local people can occasionally shop at, all the way to very exclusive ones that only expatriates and very wealthy local people can afford. Where would

Jesus shop? Whether we like it or not, where we shop does make a statement both about how we use our money, but also about how much we are trying to identify with the people we have come to serve. Unfortunately, the quality of the products available in some of the local markets and stores may not be quite up to the standard we are accustomed to, and we at times find this frustrating, but we must remember that this is the only choice most local people have and if we are going to be "with them" as Jesus was "with us" we will shop where they shop as much as possible.

Playing

Every country, every people has its own ways of relaxing and playing together. Part of fitting into a new place and becoming one with the people is learning to enjoy playing with them in every way that is morally accept-able. This frequently calls for some choices and adjustments. We may have to exchange our love of baseball and learn to play soccer; forego the tradi-tions of the Fourth of July or Thanksgiving, in exchange for the wonderful festivities of some of the local holidays; set aside our dependence on TV, videos, and movies to experience the fun of community that is at the heart of relaxation in many parts of the world. Together with the people we've come to serve—that's the goal.

Worshiping

You may never have thought much about it, but the truth is that worship is actually a very cultural event. That's hard to believe when most of the wor-ship services you've ever attended all looked pretty much alike, but there are really very few "rules" that govern worship practices worldwide. Even a brief tour through the Bible and history will show you that there are many ways that Christians pray, experience music, and show reverence to God. Identifying with the people in worship means that we allow, and even en-courage people to worship God in ways that may be very different from our way, but that are relevant and meaningful to them. Removing one's shoes before entering a house of worship is an important part of showing respect and reverence in some cultures; chanting may be more meaningful than singing; prostrating oneself in prayer better than standing or kneeling, etc. So, just as Jesus worshiped in the synagogues of Israel and followed the other religious practices that had become a part of normal Jewish worship in his day, we also allow people to worship God in ways that feel appropriate and meaningful to them.

But How!?

In this chapter we have looked at the question of incarnational ministry and what its implications are in the life of a missionary. It sounds good, right? But how do we really *do* it?

To consider how it is accomplished we have to look at the "other side" of incarnation. We started out by thinking about Jesus—how he became one with the people and thus became our example. Galatians 2:20 points us in the direction of how we can follow in His footsteps. "Christ lives in me. The life I live...I live by faith in the Son of God who loved me and gave himself for me." If Christ is living in me, HE enables me to become one with the people. John 15:5 further reminds us that only as we are abiding in Christ (the vine and the branches) can we bear any fruit. It is knowing Christ and experiencing His love intimately, having him "in us" that then compels us to serve as he did (2 Cor. 5:14). And finally, Paul reminds us that we "can do all things through Christ who strengthens us." (Phil. 4:13) Not I, but Christ—that's the foundation of incarnational mission.

So that's the good news: He who called you will live in you and enable you to live in a way that will build bridges, not barriers.

 Your Turn

1. How would you feel about someone who came to live in your country and made absolutely no effort to "fit in"? How would you feel about someone who not only made no effort to fit in, but was almost arrogant about being different and maintained his separateness? How would you feel about someone who made some basic efforts to adjust and adapt to your country? Which one would it be easier to become friends with?

2. Of the areas of identification mentioned, which do you feel will be the easiest for you? Why? Which will be most difficult? Why?

3. What are some practical things you can do to make the difficult ones easier?

Learning the Language

In the last chapter we talked about the whole concept of incarnation—becoming one with the people we are living with. As you discovered, this type of ministry affects every aspect of our life. But there is one more area that is perhaps the most important of all for a missionary who is seeking to follow Jesus' example: language learning.

Think about It

Can you imagine what it would have been like if Jesus had brought a translator from heaven and preached all his sermons and taught all his lessons through a translator for 30 years? Strange thought, huh? Being able to communicate with people in their own language is *very* much a part of incarnation, of being *together* with the people.

Reasons for Learning the Language

So, why is it so important for us to learn as much of the language as we can? Here are the most important reasons:
- It is the foundation of identification and bonding.
- It breaks down barriers.
- It increases your efficiency at doing your job.
- It's the only way to truly communicate and reach people's hearts.
- It's the only way to ever really understand the culture and the people.
- It's the only way to really know what's going on.

Myths about Language Learning

I realize, however, that learning a language is easier said than done. Not only is it a challenge, but frequently you will hear a lot of "reasons" given why going to all the trouble to learn the language is not really necessary, or not possible or practical.

• You don't need to study, you'll just "pick it up."
• You really don't need it, most people you'll deal with speak English.
• You can just use a translator.

But you guessed right. These reasons soon prove not to be true. Here is why. Very few people just "pick up" a language. Most of us need some help—a proper language school being the best option, but a trained or experienced tutor a few hours a day can also work well. The bottom line is that initially you need to be intentional about learning language and have someone experienced to guide you.

While it is true that in many places many of the local people speak English (or French or German or whatever) fluently, the reality is that for most of them this is not their mother tongue, and may, in fact, be the language associated with a colonial power. Their "heart language" is still the language they learned at their mother's knee and will always be the most significant language to them. To truly identify with them (plus others who don't speak the second language at all) we need to make an effort to reach them in their "heart language."

It is true that institutions in many places have gifted translators who can be of great help to you. But a translator is always an unconscious barrier between you and the people with whom you are wishing to communicate. To be truly "together with them" you need to be able to speak to them in their first language.

How to Learn a New Language

Since learning the language of the people is so important, how, then, can you go about it? You are probably thinking by this time that this is a pretty unrealistic expectation. You may be planning to serve for only a year or two, so how are going to learn a language in a short amount of time? Well, it is amazing how much language you can learn in a short amount of time if you really set your mind to it.

To begin with, you need to have a positive attitude—"I think I can..." (And you really can—honest!) In addition, it helps to really be convinced of the importance of language. That will keep you going on rough days! It also helps to be a bit childlike. We set our adult pride aside and become willing to make mistakes and "play" with the language, knowing we won't be perfect at first. This obviously involves being a risk-taker—something that is a *must* for learning a language. Sooner or later you just have to stick your neck out and say something that very well may create some confusion or laughter at first, but at the same time will earn you the appreciation and respect of the local people, because you are making the effort to become one with them.

Tips for Language Learning

Here are a few practical suggestions for starting to learn a language.

Use a native speaker to guide you as a tutor or informant.

Practice "active listening"—really focusing on the sounds you hear swirling around you at first. This naturally involves some serious concentration—listening for sounds and ultimately words. Remember your brain can't help you create the new sounds until it has truly heard them.

Find ways to get "comprehensible input." What does that mean? It means you need to find people who will treat you like a child, speaking "motherese" to you—the simplified, repetitive language we speak to children, accompanied with lots of body language to make it comprehensible.

Focus on all aspects of the language—beginning with listening. As an adult, however, you can benefit by learning the writing system early on so that you can get input from reading as well as listening.

Pray for the Lord's blessing on your efforts.

Well, there you have it. You can learn a language. You can come closer to people's hearts by speaking to them in their own heart language. You can experience the joys of being able to really communicate in a new language. Go for it!

1. How many languages do you already know?

2. How did you learn them?

3. Can you use those same principles to help you learn another language?

Reality Check

So here you are—almost "on your way". Probably you're planning what and how to pack, looking ahead to the unknown and exciting adventure you're facing. Naturally you have dreams and expectations of what you'll encounter when you get "over there" (wherever that may be) dreams that are based on many things. When I was a kid I read lots of mission stories and made up my mind at age 9 that I wanted to be a missionary. My dreams of mission began a very long time ago. What about you? When did you begin to develop missionary dreams? Like me, you may have read stories that whetted your appetite for mission. Maybe you listened to missionaries on furlough or student missionaries who came to your home church or academy. Maybe your interest is more recent, stemming from the urging of a friend or the urging of the Holy Spirit in your devotions or in a meeting. No matter where they began, however, now you're getting ready to turn those dreams into reality. Praise the Lord!

Having dreams is valuable, actually indispensable, for a missionary. But dreams have to be balanced by reality or they can end up disappointing—even mocking us—leading to dissatisfaction and ultimate disillusionment. So, let's take a look at a few areas that we'll face in what we'll call a "reality check".

The Place

Going to a new place, we naturally have certain ideas about what it will be like, how it will look, etc. Without really thinking too much about it, many of us expect all mission fields to look kind of alike—tropical paradises with white sand and palm trees, simple thatch and bamboo houses nestled in an exotic jungle, and of course dugout canoes for transportation. Sound familiar? We may *know* better, but this mental image lingers on.

The reality is that mission fields come in all sizes and shapes. And in today's world, because the majority of the world's population live in megacities, this of course means that the greatest mission fields are the world's cities. And cities are much the same the world over—big, crowded, dirty, and (by some standards, at least) ugly. They may be tropical and we may see a few palm trees, but somehow cities just don't fit our "mission field" stereotype. The question we have to ask ourselves, then, as we look at reality is: Are cities less of a mission field than jungles? Is a modern suburb full of people who have no knowledge of Jesus less in need of the gospel than an isolated village? The obvious answer is *no*! But ending up in a sprawling city with its inherent challenges just doesn't initially fit our dream of what a mission field is. The first reality is that a mission field is anywhere that people need to know the Lord—even a city!

Ourselves

A second area to look at is ourselves as "real missionaries". As a kid, my stereotyped "real missionary" was the pith-helmet-clad semi-saint with a tattered picture roll permanently tucked under his or her arm, perpetually hiking through jungles. The reality is that today's missionaries have probably never seen a pith helmet and would laugh at the thought of being semi-saints. Missionaries are ordinary people who happen to be working in cross-cultural settings far from home.

Naturally, most missionaries would aspire to be new, improved versions of their former selves, but unfortunately, becoming a missionary doesn't necessarily make us any different. We will almost certainly have the same basic personality traits—good and bad—we've always had. We'll have similar temptations and struggles, strengths and weaknesses. We don't suddenly become immune to the challenges of life just because we move to a new place as missionaries. The reality is that one of the beauties of God's plan is that He takes us just as we are (warts and all) and uses us in His service. Oh, He definitely works on us along the way, as we let Him, but we shouldn't be shocked or disillusioned if we find that we are still basically the same person we've always been when we arrive in the mission field, not some super- (or even semi-super) saint. God won't be surprised. Neither should we! That's the second reality.

The Work and People

The third area to consider is the work and the people to which we are called. Again we have those images in our dreams from the past—rows of adoring children hanging on our every word; droves of people welcoming us with open arms; ourselves teaching or baptizing throngs of eager new converts. Of course, such events do still take place in mission today; and I can guarantee you that you will meet and make friends with some of the most wonderful people on earth—people that you will grow to love; people you will miss immensely when you have to leave.

However, your encounters will be somewhat different from that stereotyped image you may have. Much of what we will do may be in areas where the work has been going for many years and is already well-established. We frequently serve in a supportive role, working in an already-established institution or organization. Unfortunately we may also inherit some challenges that have grown out of misunderstandings from the past. Remember, the people where you will serve have already had many encounters with Westerners—missionaries and others—before you arrived on the scene. Some of these encounters have been positive. Unfortunately, others have not. The scars left from some of these not-so-positive past encounters frequently cause attitudes of distrust and even dislike for foreigners today. We therefore may at times face (or at least sense) caution, distrust, antagonism, and occasionally, outright hatred. In addition, nationalism may at times cause people to have an anti-Western spirit which may lead to a "Yankee go home!" attitude.

If something like this should happen, does that mean that we misunderstood our call? Does it mean we should respond in kind? Obviously not. We can frequently be agents of peace and good will, binding up the wounds from the past and bringing healing to broken relationships.

The Four H's of Reality

Having looked at the realities about our place of service, ourselves, and the work we will do, let's now turn to four additional areas of reality in our personal lives that we need to consider.

It's Not Home
No matter how wonderful the place you are going to serve is, it won't be *home*—at least not initially. Home is a place that is familiar, where we feel comfortable, accepted, understood, tolerated, loved, and supported. It's where we belong. Instead, in a new place we initially feel like a stranger. We

quickly realize that we are weird. Different. Alien. *We* are the foreigners! The way we talk, dress, eat, and act are all strange. We may be touched, stared at and even laughed at. At times we may feel on trial and misunderstood. And because we don't know the language or understand the culture, we frequently feel left out—conversations buzz around us, people laugh or cry, look worried or happy, and we don't feel a part of it. That's part of the reality that may lead us to do some strange things. We develop homesickness and miss things we scarcely even liked "back home" (blizzards, registration lines at college, even cafeteria food!)

It's Not a Haven

In addition, going to the mission field is not a *haven.* It's not a place to run in order to escape—problems, work, school, responsibility, rules and authority, even bad habits, friends, or temptations. The reality is that we will discover the same challenges in the mission field that we hoped to leave behind. Temptations abound. Problems are everywhere. We still have to work and carry responsibilities, and we may discover that the rules and authority of another culture are even more difficult to cope with than our own. It's true, "You can run, but you can't hide."

It's Not Heaven

Besides not being home or a haven, the mission field is also not *heaven.* What does this mean? Well, for starters it means that we won't automatically become deeply spiritual people. Flying over salt water (or driving to another country) won't bring us closer to God. We won't automatically want to get up at 4 a.m. to pray and read our Bibles. We won't automatically get holy just because we are now missionaries.

The reality is that staying close to God in many ways is as difficult overseas as it is at home. But because we are cutting ourselves off from our normal support systems and are putting ourselves "out on a limb" with God, there will certainly be increased opportunities to "taste and see that the Lord is good" if we choose to face our challenges with Him (instead of alone).

It's Not Hell

Lastly, the mission field is not *hell.* The day comes when that initial excitement has worn off, the bubble bursts, and we wake up one morning and say, "What in the world am I doing here? Why did I think this was a good idea?" Looking longingly at a calendar, time seems to stretch endlessly into the future and we wonder if we can survive another day, let alone five more months! What happened to our sense of well-being and the wonderful joy we anticipated in our dreams of mission service? What kind of reality is this? Is it worth it? The discomfort we feel is a reality we don't enjoy.

So What Do I Do?

Having looked briefly now at the four H's of reality, let's now discuss how to handle them. To begin with it is important that we expect reality to be different from our dreams and anticipation. Just being forewarned is helpful, at least it helps us avoid the unpleasant surprise of the unexpected. Along with that, we need to begin to actually expect (and enjoy) the unexpected. We frequently discover a new reality that is vastly different and even better than the one we originally expected.

Above all, start a collection of memories. Even on the darkest days when the reality seems overwhelming, there are memories to be made and remembered. After all, this truly is an adventure—possibly the greatest adventure you've had to date. Make the most of it. Lastly, keep your eyes on Jesus—the first volunteer missionary in the Christian era. Can you imagine what it was like for Him to cope with the realities of this earth? We really can't even imagine, can we? He made it, and He's promised to be with us always, so we can make it too.

In conclusion, remember that no matter how much discomfort this experience may at times bring you, you will be much closer to *true reality* during this next weeks and months than you are today. Your hometown or college are NOT reality. You are going to be reaching out to the real world where you will encounter life in all its reality—diversity, need, pain, joy, hope and fear—to a degree you've never known it. And as a result, your reality will be forever changed. Go in peace!

1. What are some ideas you have about mission and missionaries that are probably unreal stereotypes?

2. Can you think of some things you could do to develop a more realistic view?

Staying Healthy

Health of body is important to cross-cultural service. The better you feel, the better you can perform what you came to do. Your mental state is often related to how well you are doing physically. Good health contributes to happy attitudes.

Some of you are undoubtedly *too* concerned and worried about your health. You should be assured that overall you are probably at no greater risk during your time of service cross-culturally than you would be doing something similar at home. Some of you may not be concerned enough about your health. You probably need this chapter the most of all! What is crucial is that a balanced view is important to success.

Your Concerns
- What are your major health concerns?
- Have you taken time to deal with them and take the needed action?
- What do you need to do before you depart?

Your Special Needs
- Do you have any special needs in relation to your health?
- Do you require a special diet or certain foods?
- What are your allergies?
- Do you require hard-to-find medications?
- Do you need certain supplies like contact lens solution, etc.?
- Have you made plans to care for these things?

Many people are concerned about the *wrong things*.
The major health problems are usually not:
- Exotic diseases
- Tropical parasites
- Snake bites
- Large cockroaches

So what are the issues to be concerned about? Read on!

Accidents: The number-one killer for missionaries is accidents. Traffic laws and customs differ widely. Driving conditions in many countries are less than ideal. Care in driving and riding is crucial. Motorcycles are especially hazardous. Avoidance of night travel is best.

Other accidents—Building and construction accidents are also common. Use care and don't take risks.

Weather

Climate: Radical climate changes affect us physically. Many will go to very hot and/or humid climates. Lack of air conditioning and/or heating can have serious affects unless you learn to cope. If you have lost sleep because of the humidity you cannot expect to accomplish as much as you hoped. Pace yourself.

Sun: Sunburn in a tropical climate can be swift, painful, and debilitating. If you are going to be in the sun, be sure to have a sun screen. Dehydration can also be a problem and intake of adequate fluids must be planned for.

AIDS

AIDS is a major problem in many countries. Great care needs to be taken in handling the blood and bodily fluids of others. If you are doing medical and/or dental work or even just first aid, know the rules and wear gloves.

Needles: It is good to supply your own needle if you need an injection. Better yet, don't get any injections if at all possible. Blood transfusions should only be received if you have no other option. Then you should take all the precautions possible.

Illicit sex: It should go without saying for Christians that illicit sex is forbidden. Not only is it sin, but in today's world it is foolhardy and high risk behavior.

Inoculations

You will undoubtedly get a list of required immunizations/vaccinations from the organization that is sending you. By all means follow it! We are fortunate today to have vaccinations/immunizations for many diseases that were previously serious problems—cholera, typhoid, tetanus, polio, rabies, yellow fever, some types of encephalitis, meningococcal meningitis, and hepatitis A and B are the main ones. Not all of these are required for every area, so double check with your sending organization to be sure you have the ones needed for the specific area to which you are going.

Malaria

Even after we've had the necessary inoculation we know that there are still some serious illnesses we might encounter. One of the most serious ones is malaria. As you know, malaria is a very real problem in certain tropical areas. The incidence of malaria has been reduced in many areas today—especially cities; however, there are still pockets in many tropical countries where malaria continues to be a serious problem and is therefore something that cannot be taken carelessly. Fortunately, it is quite easily treated, especially if diagnosed and treated early, but hopefully can be avoided. If malaria is a common problem in the area where you will be serving (or traveling for any length of time) there are several important things you can do.

Since malaria is transmitted by a mosquito, one of the most important things you can do is try to avoid being bitten by mosquitoes. The female anopheles mosquito which carries malaria, generally bites only at night, so you should take extra precautions at night. Wear clothing that covers your legs, arms, and feet, use insect repellent (with DEET, if possible) on your skin and clothes, sleep in a protected place—either a room with good screens or under a mosquito net that has no holes and has been treated with an insect repellant.

In addition, you may want to take a prophylactic which keeps you from getting malaria even if you are bitten, especially if you are in an area where malaria is a severe problem. The most commonly prescribed prophylactic for adults at present, is Mefloquine. However, since some people have unpleasant side effects from the prophylactic, many prefer to use caution in avoiding mosquito bites, and then just treat malaria immediately and vigorously if they should get it.

Food Safety

Most of us are interested in eating on a relatively regular basis, aren't we? Thus the prospect that we may be unable to find food that is safe to eat is cause for some real concern. Due to the hot weather in many parts of the world, varying degrees of concern for following hygienic practices, and the presence of different strains of "bugs" to which our systems are not accustomed, it is true that it is easier to get sick from eating foods in a new place than it is at home. So, what can we do?

Aside from preparing all your own food, (a pretty unrealistic idea) what can you do? Since most bacteria that cause illness are destroyed by heat, one of the best guidelines is to eat food that is well-cooked—preferably eating it "hot off the griddle". Since much food is prepared on the spot, this is a real possibility. Foods that are dry are also much less likely to be contaminated than foods that are moist (especially if they are prepackaged and sealed.)

Some Things to Avoid:

- Raw foods (salads, pre-peeled fruits, etc.)
- Foods with a high sugar content—they provide a good culture for bacteria to grow in, especially if they are warm and moist
- Food that has been sitting around uncovered, thus inviting flies and other insects to land on it with their contaminated feet
- Milk products that are not from companies that are known to follow hygienic procedures in the processing

It's true that the local people and some of the "old time" missionaries may eat all kinds of things that you probably should not eat—especially when you first arrive. Your immune system is not ready to deal with a lot of new "critters" at first. Gradually you will probably develop some immunities that will enable you to be a bit more adventuresome, but "being safe rather than sorry" is good advice for a newcomer.

In most areas the major food problem is *not* contaminated food. It is water and liquids. Rarely is the "natural" water safely drinkable. Untreated water often contains harmful bacteria, viruses, and parasites such as amoeba that can cause serious and/or long-term problems.

Drinking Water and Other Fluids
Bottled water: It can be a solution, depending where you get the bottles! In some places, even the local bottled water is not safe.

Ice: Unfortunately the same holds true for local ice. On a hot day it may be hard to resist, but you may regret your indulgence.

Water Safety

An additional area of concern is the water supply. It is very important for you to drink a lot of liquid, but at the same time, the water supply in many places is less-than-safe. What can you do?

- Use some kind of chemical treatment on the water. Various kinds of water purification tablets are on the market and most work fairly well if they are fresh. I often used a solution of iodine called Lugol's solution during my missionary itinerating days in Asia. You can also use Clorox bleach. One capful of bleach per 2 gallons of water should fix things.
- Boil the water. Be sure that it comes to a rolling boil and stays that way for at least 10 minutes.
- Buy bottled water if you can find some that is safe. (Buy only bottles that are sealed, from companies that have a reputation for safety.)
- Drink bottled drinks—especially sodas from international companies that have a worldwide reputation to protect.
- Drink tea—In many countries "tea" (which may be made from real tea leaves or various and sundry other plants) is a very safe alternative to water. It has been boiled, is usually very weak, and is in covered containers so tends to be safe.

What to Do if You Get Diarrhea

Though it is important for you to take reasonable precautions, the chances are that at some time you'll probably get some kind of a gastro-intestinal upset. The most common type is referred to as "travelers diarrhea", a self-limited illness that lasts a few days and is most commonly caused by a form of *e-coli* bacteria. Having diarrhea is never pleasant or convenient, but it can actually be a good thing since it is the body's way of getting rid of "the bad guys". The most important thing for you to do initially, then, is to avoid getting dehydrated. If you are able to drink liquids this is very important. Keep drinking (or sipping if you are also nauseated).

Rehydration drink (see the recipe below) is good if packets or bottles of commercially-prepared rehydration fluids are not available. If the symptoms continue for more than two days (in adults), or if symptoms of serious dehydration occur, you may need to see a doctor (if one is available) or bring out the "bigger guns"—antibiotics (e.g. Cipro, Bactrim, etc.) and medication that stops the symptoms by stopping the diarrhea (e.g. Pepto Bismol, Imodium, Lomotil). Obviously, any diarrhea that continues longer than a few days, or is accompanied by bloody stools and/or fever should be treated by a doctor, and may even require hospitalization.

Oral Rehydration Drink

1 liter of purified (boiled, if necessary) water
2 Tablespoons of sugar
1/4 teaspoon of salt
1/4 teaspoon of bicarbonate of soda (or another 1/4 tsp. of salt if bicarbonate of soda is not available)
1/2 cup of orange juice or a squeeze of lemon (for potassium replacement and taste)

Crime
Violent crime is probably less likely in most places than it is in North America. On the other hand rip-offs, scams, and petty theft abound in many places. Your mental health can be ruined temporarily by such things.

Women: In many places women who go places alone are considered fair game. There is safety in numbers. Don't be presumptuous and test your guardian angels!

Taxis: Both men and women should be cautious when taking taxis. Whether the motive is robbery or rape, taxi drivers have been known to take advantage of foreigners in many countries. Traveling in groups is an obvious precaution. Avoiding taxi travel at night is another. And for women, *never* getting into a taxi alone is very wise advice.

A Sample First Aid Kit

Here is what Maranatha Volunteers International suggests to its groups to take along on a short term mission project. Ideally, a physician is a member of your group and can attend to medical needs within your group. Some groups may have a nurse with them. Others have people skilled in various levels of medical expertise. Certainly a first aid kit should be part of the group luggage. Items to be included in a standard first aid kit include:

- Antibiotics (although it is expensive and requires a prescription, Cipro is preferred because it covers the major dysentery pathogens—except amoebas, it is not sun sensitive like some antibiotics, and there are few side effects).
- Ace bandage strips
- Aloe Vera or anything with Benzocaine (for severe sunburn)
- Aspirin
- Band aids
- Bandages—telfa pads and tape
- Benadryl

- Cling tape (optional)
- Cotton balls
- Female hygiene items
- Gloves (always wear them when handling blood, etc.)
- Hydrogen peroxide or Betadine (for sterilizing/ cleaning)
- Insect repellant with DEET, 30% strength
- Motrin or Advil (for sore muscles that aren't accustomed to working quite this hard or in this way)
- Needles (to clean out dirt and sand under the skin)
- Pepto Bismol (for first stages of intestinal blowouts)
- Polysporin (skin ointment for infections)
- Saline solution (for eye wash)
- Sore throat lozenges (from cold morning air, eating dust, too much talking, etc.)
- Steri-strips (optional)
- Sun screen (minimum of SPF 15; SPF 30-45 is preferred)

First Aid Medications

Cold Medicines

Tussi-Organidin: Non-narcotic syrup.

Hucotuss: Narcotic cough syrup, will cause drowsiness.

Ru-Tuss: Antihistamine/Decongestant non-sedative, 3 times a day.

Ventolin Inhaler: For asthma or allergic breathing problems, two huffs every hour as needed.

Anti-Itch Medicines

Benadryl: Antihistamine, for hives, causes drowsiness, 1-2 every 6 hours.

Lidex Cream: For non-fungal itchy rashes, 2-3 times a day.

Lotrimin Cream: Fungal rashes like athletes foot, 2 times a day.

Pain Medicines

Anaprox DS: Non-narcotic analgesic/anti-inflammatory/headache, may cause ulcers, take with food, 2-3 times a day.

Vicodin: Narcotic analgesic, causes drowsiness, 1-2 every 6 hours.

Water Safety

Water purification tablets

Stomach Problems
    Tagamet: Ulcer pain, also non-sedating anti-itch pill, 2 times a day.
    Imodium: Anti-diarrheal, 1 tablet after each stool, maximum of 12 per day. Allow nature to clear toxin form body prior to use.
    Compazine: Anti-nausea, use only after stomach contents empty and still retching, 1 tablet every 6 hours.

Antibiotics (Note: allergies do occur)
    PCE: Erythromycin, good for bronchitis, skin, strep throat, 2 times a day.
    Amoxil: Penicillin, good for elderly with bronchitis, bladder infections, 3 times a day.
    Cipro: Broad spectrum antibiotic, good for bacterial diarrhea, skin infections, serious infections like pneumonia, 2 times a day. NOTE: may cause diarrhea.

From: *Maranatha Guide to Adventure.*

An Important Resource

Centers for Disease Control and Prevention. *Health Information for International Travel* (there is an updated edition each year). Atlanta, Georgia: U.S. Department of Health and Human Services. Public Health Service. HHS Publication No. (CDC) 95-8280. This is the most authoritative source of information on health concerns in international travel. For updates check the CDC website http://www.cdc.gov.

Remember that the best places to find out any special information about immunizations and particular health advice are your mission organization, your physician, travel clinic, or health department. Immunizations may be required for entry into some countries.

Resources for Further Study

Axtell, R. E., ed. (1993). *Do's and Taboos around the World.* (3rd ed.) New York, NY: John Wiley & Sons, Inc.

Aroney-Sine, C. (1994). *Survival of the Fittest: Keeping Yourself Healthy in Travel and Service Overseas.* Monrovia, CA: MARC.

Brewster, T., & Brewster, B. S. (1984). *Language Learning Is Communication, Is Ministry.* Pasadena, CA: Lingua House.

Haines, M., & Thorowgood, S., eds. (1998). *The Traveller's Healthbook.* London, UK: WEXAS International.

Historical Sketches of the Foreign Mission of the Seventh-day Adventists. (1985 reprint; original 1886). Payson, AZ: Leaves-of-Autumn Books.

Kohls, L. R. (1996). *Survival Kit for Overseas Living for Americans Planning to Live and Work Abroad.* Yarmouth, ME: Intercultural Press.

Schubert, E. (1993). *What Missionaries Need to Know about Burnout and Depression.* New Castle, IN: Olive Branch Publications.

Werner, D., Thuman, C., & Maxwell, J. (1992). *Where There Is No Doctor: A Village Health Care Handbook.* (Rev. ed.) Berkeley, CA: The Hesperian Foundation.

PART **5** PASSPORT TO MISSION

Sharing Christ in a Different Culture

18

Building Redemptive Relationships

Because a missionary or a witness is what we are, rather than what we do, it becomes a twenty four-hour-a-day, seven-day-a-week activity. We are witnessing by the way we dress, by our activities, by our values, and by our priorities. The question of a "target audience," a specific group of people with whom you wish to share Jesus, is almost beside the point. Your "target audience" is everybody around you, particularly those your life touches in normal activity. In this chapter you will begin to identify natural avenues for discipling and natural environments in which to witness.

 Think about It

People around you are aware, at least subconsciously, of your values and thus, your loyalties. Stop and reflect on the past 24 hours: What does your clothing, right now, say about your values and self-image? Has your behavior today been seen as patient, kind and considerate? What parts of your behavior have been seen as impatient, inconsiderate and unkind? How have your priorities, today, valued others more than yourself?

Discipling

You may need to add a new term to your vocabulary, one that your spell-checker will not recognize: "discipling." Discipling means witnessing to others so they become new Christians or new disciples of Jesus. It involves the entire process from spiritual conception to new birth, and on to becoming a fully mature, self-reproducing Christian. This work does not belong to the pastor, it is *your* responsibility. Remember, it is not the *shepherds* who produce new sheep. *Sheep* make new sheep. Just so, it is not pastors who make new disciples. It is disciples who make new disciples. There are very good reasons for this:

1. You are the one who got to know the person who is becoming a Christian in the first place.
2. You are the one who has introduced the new disciple to Jesus.
3. You are the one the new Christian knows and trusts.
4. You are the most believable example of genuine Christianity the new disciple knows.
5. It is the most natural for the new Christian to learn the faith by observing and copying you.
6. This obviously will keep you on your toes as a growing Christian.

Exercise:

On this page you see a group of boxes labeled by the areas of your normal life, boxes in which you generally live and work. This is your personal "network", and, as you will see, evangelism or Christian witness operates best as "network" evangelism.

Within each box write the names of people you meet and talk to at least 3 to 4 times a week. These are your primary contacts for Jesus. They are the people who know and trust you, who feel comfortable with you. These are people with whom natural channels of communication have been established. Some degree of relationship has already been established with these people. The issue now is to translate these into redemptive relationships.

Home and Family	*Work*
Associations	*Neighbors & Friends*

For many of us, especially longtime Christians, we may find that there are very few names in our *boxes* that are not already Christians. What can you do to enlarge the number of *potentially* redemptive relationships? The answer is twofold: be more friendly and make more friends.

How to Relate to Others

As you think about how you can become a more effective soul winner consider this statement about the master soulwinner.

Christ's method alone will give true success in reaching the people. The Savior mingled with men as one who desired their good. He showed His sympathy for them ministered to their needs and won their confidence. Then he bade them "Follow me."
Ellen G. White, *Ministry of Healing*, 143.

Here are some practical guidelines for relating to others. Begin practicing these today in all your contacts.

Develop good listening skills—Practice focusing on what people are saying to you, not on what you want to say in return or rebuttal. Listen attentively and ask for clarification.

Establish personal rapport—Work on face to face contact, close proximity with eye contact and even physical contact. Caution, eye contact may be viewed differently in some cultures.

Foster an attitude of encouragement—Make people feel good, affirm their good ideas and plans. Don't nag! As the song says, "accent the positive and de-emphasize the negative."

Make yourself interesting to others by being interested in them—Be aware of current events, books, films, and music. Develop hobbies that you can share with others. Ask others about themselves. Focus on *them*, what they do and why, their families, jobs, interests, and what makes life exciting to them. Get them to tell their "story."

Secrets of Effective Witnessing

Earn the right to be a witness by first being a genuine friend. Be natural. Don't attempt to be what you are not. The real you will come through anyway. Don't step in and out of a role.

Don't rush. Remember that there are two ways to get a chicken out of an egg: with a hammer or a little warmth and time. Stimulate interest that leads to questions, then answer them. Be obvious without being offensive. Be a deliberate Christian without making a "big deal" out of it.

Draw attention to the multi-culturalism of Christianity. It is originally an Asian faith with African connections.

Make your point without demanding agreement. People need time and space to reflect on life-changing paradigm shifts.

Jesus saw in every soul one to whom must be given the call to His kingdom. He reached the hearts of the people by going among them as one who desired their good. He sought them in the public streets, in private homes, on the boats, in the synagogue, by the shores of the lake, and at the marriage feast. He met them at their daily vocations and manifested an interest in their secular affairs. Ellen G. White, *Desire of Ages*, 151.

Ideas for Expanding the Boxes"

- Take a class (or teach) at a local school or university.
- Join a musical group.
- Join and participate in professional organizations
- Join and participate in service clubs (e.g. Rotary, Kiwanis, etc.). Many of them are international.
- Attend neighborhood events. Often you do not need an invitation to attend weddings, funerals, baptisms, fiestas, work groups, or sporting events.
- Places to meet people: cafés and coffee houses, tea houses, local markets, fairs and festivals, plazas and parks, book stores and stalls, flea markets, sporting events, recreation and game areas for soccer games, bird collectors, open-air chess, bocci-ball, etc., etc., etc.
- Note: Be cautious about identifying with political groups or activities.

Remember the can of soup? The more we "open the can of soup," and eat it, the easier it is to share it. Think of the last time you discovered a great new restaurant or a fantastic recipe for pizza. Remember the last time you fell in love. Remember how easy it was to tell others about it?

1. We have talked about being a witness for Jesus. Who is your primary audience right now? How are you witnessing to them? List *three steps* you can take *this week* to add non-Christian contacts to your boxes.

2. Can you remember a time when you offended someone to whom you were witnessing? How would you do it better today?

3. Have you ever sensed that you were God's mouth, feet, or hands so that sharing Jesus simply flowed naturally? What happened? Why?

Preparing Your Testimony

"God has not retained many of us as lawyers, but he has summoned all of us as witnesses."

As they flew from Amsterdam to Bombay, an Asian gentleman and a Western missionary shared a number of hours of conversation over the usual topics: the airline food, current events and world conditions, family and work. After a pause the Asian with a turban mentioned that he was returning home for the birthday of Guru Nanak, the last of the great gurus of Sikhism. It was an important date for him and his family and he returned home from London annually for the event. He went on to describe the basic tenets of the Sikh faith and how it permeated his entire life from the clothing he wore to the annual celebrations. Then, turning to look the missionary in the eyes, he asked, "Now tell me about Christianity. What do you believe?" *The missionary reflected for a moment in prayer and replied....*

Think about It

Everyone faces opportunities such as this and must be ready "in season and out of season" to share his or her faith. Where would you begin to answer the Sikh's question? How would his background and faith determine what you would say or how you would couch it? Would your testimony be factual (intellectual, cognitive, doctrinal) or personal (relational, affective)? Why?

How to Become a Missionary

Jesus and his disciples arrived on the other side of Lake Galilee, in the territory of Gerasa. As soon as Jesus got out of the boat, he was met by a man who came out of the burial caves there. This man had an evil spirit in him and lived among the tombs. Nobody could keep him tied with chains any more; many times his feet and his hands had been tied, but every time he broke the chains and smashed the irons on his feet. He was too strong for anyone to control him. Day and night he wandered among the tombs and through the hills, screaming and cutting himself with stones.

He was some distance away when he saw Jesus; so he ran, fell on his knees before him, and screamed in a loud voice, "Jesus, Son of the Most High God! What do you want with me? For God's sake, I beg you, don't punish me." (He said this because Jesus was saying, "Evil spirit, come out of this man!")

So Jesus asked him, "What is your name?"

The man answered, "My name is 'Mob'–there are so many of us!" And he kept begging Jesus not to send the evil spirits out of that region.

There was a large herd of pigs near by, feeding on a hillside. So the spirits begged Jesus, "Send us to the pigs, and let us go into them." He let them go, and the evil spirits went out of the man and entered the pigs. The whole herd–about two thousand pigs in all–rushed down the side of the cliff into the lake and was drowned.

The men who had been taking care of the pigs ran away and spread the news in the town and among the farms. People went out to see what had happened, and when they came to Jesus, they saw the man who used to have the mob of demons in him. He was sitting there, clothed and in his right mind; and they were all afraid. Those who had seen it told the people what had happened to the man with the demons, and about the pigs.

So they asked Jesus to leave the territory.

As Jesus was getting into the boat, the man who had had the demons begged him, "Let me go with you!"

But Jesus would not let him. Instead, he told him, "Go back home to your family and tell them how much the Lord has done for you and how kind he has been to you."

So the man left and went all through the Ten Towns, telling what Jesus had done for him. And all who heard it were amazed. (Mark 5:1-20 TEV)

Think about this former demoniac who is now a "missionary" to his own people. What sort of tools or budget did this new "missionary" have? How much training did this new "missionary" have? What do you think he said to his family and friends? What were the two components of Jesus' instructions to him? How would these two components look in your story?

Your Own Story

Your story is as real, important and unique as the story of the healed demoniac. He could not tell the story of others, since he probably didn't know any. He probably was not even Jewish and had no part in the history of God's covenant people. Each person's story is unique, personal and an account of grace in action.

Remember that witnesses are allowed to tell only what they have seen and experienced. They are not teachers or specialists who are expected to be theological authorities. Remember also that secondhand information is never as reliable as firsthand. In court, secondhand information is never accepted.

You may be a convert with an amazing story of being rescued from a terrible life of sin. Or you may be a "born and bred Christian" who has never known a life apart from Jesus and has never even been tempted to wander from your allegiance to Jesus. Both of these stories are important, grace-filled, and part of the larger picture of what God is doing in this world.

Preparing Your Own Testimony

How do you prepare your own testimony? To get started, return to your life map in chapter 8 and reflect for a bit on who you are, where you have come from, and what you have been through. You may wish to redraw the spiritual "map" of your life with "geographical" events such as mountains for high experiences, deserts of despair, flooded rivers of trials, and gardens of delight. Bridges may represent people who have helped you over impasses. Remember, your experience and your life with Jesus are the basis for your testimony.

Your Life Map

Near to God

Far from God

Childhood   Present

Here are some common components to a personal testimony:
- Where my story begins
- What my life was like without Jesus
- How and where I met Jesus. Who introduced me to Jesus? Any unusual features about the event?
- What changed when I met Jesus and invited Him into my life as Lord and Savior?
- How is my life different now than before I met Christ?
- What Jesus means to me personally and what I value most about the relationship? (Be as specific as possible here.)
- Specific biblical promises or passages that are very meaningful to me.

All of this should take no more than 3 to 4 minutes to tell.

The objective of sharing this story is to make others "jealous" of your special relationship with Jesus and to create a desire on their part to have a similar relationship.

Contextualizing Your Story

Every story teller knows that each audience is different and that the story must be "tailored" to fit the audience. Language and style will change with each audience. We call this "contextualization" because each new "context" of telling the story calls for this reshaping of your story.

This suggests that you should seriously reflect on what you know about the faith and culture of the people to whom you are going? Its history? Its main figures and personalities? Its historic relations with Christianity and the West? Possible bridges between the host faith and Christianity? All of this will be important in contextualizing or reshaping your story.

Be careful, however. Bernard Joinet tells of a well-meaning missionary who, in his attempt to identify with the people to whom he had been sent, called all the people of the village together. He professed his love for them and his determination to be one of them. To dramatize his words and decision to break with his own people, the missionary took out his passport and burned it in front of the shocked onlookers. What was meant as an act of solidarity, however, was not seen that way at all by the villagers. For them he had repudiated his own family and people. He did not, in their minds, know the meaning of love. "He rejects and despises those who gave him life," they said, "who fed and reared him. We can't trust him. He has rejected his father and mother. Perhaps one day he will also reject us whom he calls his brothers!" ("I am a Stranger in My Father's House," *African Ecclesiastical Review* 14 (1972): 244-245.)

1. Write out the major details of your story. This will help you to choose your words carefully and make it engaging.

2. Now practice telling this story or "testimony." Share it with a Christian friend and ask for his or her reaction and help in perfecting it. Then share it with a non-Christian friend or family member and ask for his or her response.

3. From what you know of your host culture, rewrite your story to make it appealing in that culture.

Leading Someone to Christ

In this chapter you will learn specific ways to introduce people to Jesus as a personal Savior.

As you think about introducing people to Jesus, where do you start? The starting point is trust. It is often very impolite to walk right in with your Bible and your Savior. This is similar to butting into an ongoing conversation without any sense of what is being discussed. The people do not know you and have no reason to trust you. Your testimony has no value until you have established your commitment to the people in a deep and accepting friendship. Before you can share Jesus you must earn the right to share Jesus. So ask yourself, "Why should they believe me?"

Before You Begin . . .

Stop and think first about the people to whom you are introducing Jesus. There are frequently significant differences between these people and the people you are used to in your own culture. These differences may include
- *Background*: family, ethnicity, nationality, education, personal history, age.
- *Shared history*: the degree to which you both have known each other and shared some of life together, schooling, job, family.
- *Core values*: stuff that is really important in this person's life, family, reputation, sports, finances.
- *Decision-making style*: individual or group decision-making orientation.
- *The manner in which they learn*: visual, audio, cognitive, affective.

Observing these factors should help you to find appropriate ways of introducing Jesus. In addition you should be aware of other significant cultural differences when you think about leading someone to Jesus.

Other Differences

1. *Motives to seek salvation*: Much of North American society is a guilt-based society. We sense personal guilt for sins and shortcomings. Other societies are shame-based. They do not have a sense of personal guilt, but rather one of collective shame. Thus they may sense their shame within their family or clan or tribe. It is not so much a personal matter, but a collective matter. Generally shame-based societies are more prone to making collective decisions and, parallel to their lack of a sense of personal guilt, they are very reticent about stepping out individually. In fact, such an individual act would produce a strong sense of shame at moving contrary to, or opposed to, their collective. Here the strongest decisions for Christ are made in the group.

2. *Where do you start?* In the Western model people are generally introduced to the Scriptures first and then to God the Father, the Son and the Holy Spirit. After that they study various doctrines and practices of the Bible as understood by the Seventh-day Adventists, as well many other Christians. In many other cultures the first question is, "How can I experience the power of God?" They want to know your own personal experience with God. Often prayer is a high-priority subject as they begin to experience the God of the Scriptures.

3. *What do you build on?* As you look for a place to connect, it may be well to ask about their sense of need? Where may their faith have failed? Are there redemptive analogies that will enable them to understand biblical concepts? Are there stories and myths, such as the "altar to the unknown god" which Paul used when speaking to the Athenians (Acts 17:22-28)?

4. *Where there is no god*: Our Western model has presupposed at least some Christian orientation, and colonialism made that orientation seemingly widespread in much of the world. People accepted Jesus because they accepted the Bible. But as many areas of the world experience either growing nationalism or become multi-cultural and secularized, that orientation is no longer so widespread. It can no longer be assumed that people have accepted the Bible as the Word of God. Other living faiths are experiencing similar confusion as Western secularism is spread through the media, particularly television. While classic Buddhism can be atheistic or godless, and is more of a philosophy, secularism is qualitatively different. Secularism is not the *denial* or God, it is the *irrelevance* of God. As in formerly Christian lands, in Buddhist, Hindu and even Islamic countries, there are growing segments of society where the faith is only a thin cultural veneer covering an essentially secular outlook on life.

5. *Order of topics*: In non-Christian cultures different presuppositions must prevail. People generally do not even have a pre-Christian orientation. Be sensitive to a priority of topics. In some situations you might follow a

sequence such as Scripture, God, Christ, Holy Spirit, etc. In other situations the sequence might be Christ, God, Holy Spirit, Scriptures, etc.

6. *Introduce them to Jesus first.* Cognitively-oriented Western Adventists are more prone to come to Jesus through belief in the Scriptures, while non-Western cultures are more prone to be relational and intuitive. It may be best to introduce people first to Jesus and after that to the Scriptures. They will accept Jesus on the basis of your testimony and they will accept the Scriptures on the basis of their commitment to Jesus.

7. *How do people become Christians?* There are at least four major paths to faith in Jesus:

The faith of the group or family. This is particularly true for many Christians who were born into Christian families. In some primal group-oriented societies, it is common (Acts 16:33; 1Cor.1:16) for whole families to convert and the conversion is generally more lasting than the conversion of one against the wishes of the family. By pressing for individual conversion you may win one but lose (alienate) many.

A relationship with a Christian. The saying is trite, but true, "Christianity is caught, not taught." If one does not have confidence in the messenger, his message may not be accepted either. The greater the distance between the messenger and the listener, the less the likelihood of developing a personal relationship of credibility and trust.

Dreams and visions. While God is more than anxious to use us in the process of winning others to faith in Jesus, he is not limited to our cooperation. As God spoke to Cornelius directly (Acts 10:1-8), he still speaks to people today. But he then often brings them in contact with his own people for further help.

Crisis event. Wars, famines, floods and other natural disasters as well as personal crises frequently result in a "failure of faith" and an openness to a new object of faith and devotion. People in the former Soviet Union, especially in central Asia, as well as in China and elsewhere experienced a vacuum of faith and meaning that had to be filled. If Christians cannot fill that void, too often it is filled by cheap substitutes (e.g. materialism, nationalism, addictions, etc.)

Most people in this world do not share our Western history or presuppositions. Issues such as differing theories of inspiration and different canonical lists, and even denominationalism are foreign and irrelevant to them. Faith is more concrete and less abstract. The important question is, "What can Jesus do for my life and my group, right now?"

Often they will accept Jesus on the basis of the testimony of your personal experience, and the clear indicators in your life of the reality of that experience. Your humble life, your spiritual commitment and faithful walk with Christ is a convincing foundation that will allow the Holy Spirit to empower anything you verbally say to them.

After Your Testimony

Once you have shared your testimony, it may be appropriate to ask your listener for his/her response. Remember there are direct and indirect societies. Moreover, in most non-Western societies, an act of commitment will require the decision of a larger group. You may wish to frame your probing accordingly:

- Does my experience of a personal God make sense in the context of your faith?
- Is an experience such as mine possible in the context of your faith?
- I don't think that my God is a local or Western God. How has he been active in your faith history?

If your friend seems particularly open to what you are saying you may wish to become more direct. Do not be afraid of a direct question. Your friend may be waiting for it. You may wish to ask your friend:

- "Jesus met these (be specific) needs in my life. Do you think he could do the same for you?"
- "Jesus has become my personal friend as well as Savior. Would you like to get acquainted with him also?"
- "Jesus has brought tremendous peace to my mind and life and enables me to cope with life's pressures. Would you like to experience that peace and help also?"

Then What?

If your friend says yes, be prepared to share some short specific "snapshot" stories about Jesus (e.g. the woman at the well, the woman taken in adultery, Jesus with the children, the rich young ruler, the wedding feast, etc.).

If the setting is appropriate, invite your friend to pray with you. The prayer should include something similar to:

- "Jesus, I have just heard about you and this is new to me...."
- "Jesus, I am willing to give you a chance in my life...."
- "Jesus, I want to get to know you better...."
- "Jesus, I invite you into my life and I ask you to help me with...."

Some people are nervous about praying, and they may be afraid that they will say the wrong thing and offend God. You may wish to lead them through a prayer, inviting them to repeat it after you. Here is a sample prayer.

Lord Jesus, I have just heard about you and I want to know you. I want you to take away my faults and failures and accept me as your own child. Please come into my heart and mind, as you have promised, and lead my life in this difficult world. Amen.

Some Helpful Scriptures

Here are some passages of Scriptures that might be helpful to share with your friend(s). Remember that these are offered not on the basis that Scripture is more important than Jesus, but that these are Jesus' own words to his "followers."

- Revelation 3:20 "Behold I stand at the door and knock...."
- John.1:12 "To those who accept me, I give power...."
- John 6:37 "Everyone whom the Father gives me will come to me; I will certainly not reject anyone who comes to me."

If Your Friend Hesitates

If your friend hesitates, he or she does not necessarily reject you or Jesus. It may mean that your friend needs more time to think about it, time to talk with others about it, time to be polite in his or her response, or any number of things.

It is important for you to give your friend the opportunity to think about what you have said. It may be very new. It may be totally outside his or her realm of plausibility. If this person is your friend, then you will continue to be a friend and allow time and space for your friend to reflect and begin what may be a lengthy decision-making process.

Ask your pastor for the opportunity to join him in an evangelistic Bible study, and, if appropriate, to teach one yourself.

Urban Living: A Guide for the Beginner

More and more missionaries are called to live and work in cities along with over 50% of the world population. Here are ten suggestions to help you in living and working in the city.

- Subscribe to a good local newspaper and keep abreast of what is happening in your city.
- Find a good local radio station. Check the billboards and subway ads for what is hot. Information is very important.
- Join a health club or spa. It is a great place to meet people.
- Get to know your neighborhood. Shop locally, take walks, talk with people. Ask them where they come from, how the neighborhood has changed, where to get good help and repairs.
- Join Kiwanis or Rotary. They are always recruiting new members and it provides instant friendships and connections. It is worth the expense.
- Be aware of what is current in the media: TV, movies, books, etc. You want to sound intelligent.
- Urban friendships are generally shallow and transient. It takes time for people to learn to trust you.
- Learn the history of your city. Why is it there? Who settled where and when? What is the political history? The economic history? Who has been in charge?
- Urban people generally love their city. Don't disparage it. Enjoy it!
- Learn to root for the home teams!

21

Helping Christians Grow

If you don't care where you are going, it doesn't matter which direction you take. If you don't care about the finished product, it doesn't matter how you build the design. Because we do care, it is helpful to attempt to envision the final project as you begin to lead the new believer toward a mature faith. In this chapter the student will explore the more difficult and important work of helping the new Christian integrate his life and faith.

Think about It

What do you think? What do mature believers look like? What do they believe? How do they live? Why do you have this picture? Where did you get this picture?

Discipleship

How does one identify a Christian, a disciple of Jesus? Jesus spoke of four essential marks of his followers:

1. A disciple identifies with the person of Jesus, denying self, taking up the cross and following Jesus. (Luke 9:23)
2. A disciple is obedient to the word of Jesus, faithfully holding to Jesus' teaching and living it. (John 8:31,32)
3. A disciple expresses and demonstrates love for all other disciples. (John 13:35)
4. A disciple is fruitful in the work of Jesus, producing more disciples. (John 15:8-16)

As you work with new Christians you must model these essential marks and enable your friend(s) to model them also. But we need to explore some indicators of these four marks as they become more fully developed.

Eight Major Indicators of a Mature Faith

The recent Valuegenesis study analyzing the maturity level of young people in the Seventh-day Adventist Church is a useful tool for our purposes. It identified eight major indicators of a mature faith. While these are expressed in very North American terms, they can be translated into a variety of cultural contexts.

1. Trusting in God's saving grace and believing firmly in the humanity and divinity of Jesus.
2. Experiencing a sense of personal well-being, security and peace.
3. Integrating faith and life, seeing work, family, social relationships, and political choices as part of one's religious life.
4. Seeking spiritual growth through study, reflection, prayer, and discussion with others.
5. Seeking to be part of a community of believers in which people give witness to their faith which supports and nourishes one another.
6. Holding life-affirming values, including commitment to racial and gender equality.
7. Advocating social and global change to bring about greater social justice.
8. Serving humanity consistently and passionately through acts of love and justice.

Some of these indicators are more obvious than others, some are more easily achieved than others. These indicators are not provided as a basis for immediate judgment, but as goals toward which mentors encourage their disciples to move.

How to Encourage Growth in New Christians

As you disciple new Christians and seek to move them toward a mature, self-reproducing faith, you may wish to help them focus on the following:

The lordship of Christ—Jesus Christ must truly be the Lord of the believers' lives. Growing in faith they must be captivated by the person of Jesus and surrender major areas of life to Jesus' control: their careers, marriage plans, families, possessions.

Bible study—Young believers need to learn to daily read and enjoy the Bible, to study it personally and with others in a group, and to memorize meaningful passages. With individual help, young believers soon learn to feed themselves. The process may take a few years.

Prayer and devotion to God—They need to learn to pray and have a meaningful quiet time of worship daily. They should also be taught to pray for others (a simple prayer list may help), how to confess sins and to live a life of thanksgiving.

Fellowship and the church—Believers grow in the context of fellowship with other believers. New believers need to belong. They need to learn that the church is their spiritual family (cf. the "one another" passages of the New Testament).

Christian character— Paul labored hard to "present everyone mature in Christ" (Col.1:28). Paul's goal of Christlikeness is the most essential aspect of discipleship training. This is a lifelong process that builds on the abiding essentials of faith, hope and love.

Relationships—Discipleship affects all interpersonal relationships (e.g. between family members, employers and employees, the church leaders and members). New believers need to be taught how to apply gospel principles to their relationship with people in the context of their own culture.

Witnessing—Missionaries should teach young believers to share their faith with members of their own family and with friends. This is the most fertile soil for ongoing, fruitful evangelism and church planting.

Social justice—Growing Christians need to learn that the Christian life is personal but never privatized. Christians must therefore be concerned about sinful social structures and minister also to the hungry, the homeless, the oppressed and marginalized.

(Adapted and expanded from Lewis, Jonathan, ed. [1993] *Working Your Way to the Nations: A Guide to Effective Tentmaking*. Pasadena, CA: William Carey Library.)

A Journey Together

Obviously this type of mature faith will take time to develop. As you look at these eight indicators, you may sense a need for growth yourself. As you "disciple" a new Christian, you should begin by confessing that you are still growing also. You may be only a step ahead of the new disciple. But you know where you both are going and how to get there.

Let's think about how to model and teach new Christians in four essential practices of a growing Christian life.

Prayer

Since you are the first model of Christianity for the new Christian, your prayer life becomes a model for his or her prayer life. By instruction and by praying together you introduce the person to different forms of prayer.

Conversation with God—Prayer is the opening of the heart to God as to a friend. Nothing is hidden from God. Everything can be discussed. Nothing will embarrass God, drive Him away, or make Him angry.

Worship—In a worship setting prayer is often less personal and more a matter of bringing the community collectively to the throne of God.

Meditation—Prayer is not simply bringing a "shopping list" to God, it is praise and thanksgiving as well as sitting quietly and listening to the voice of God, "when every other voice is hushed." (Ministry of Healing, page 58)

Many forms—Prayer can take on many forms: letter writing, singing, and playing instruments. David danced. Cultures differ in the ways people approach God meaningfully.

Bible Study

The Scriptures are the record of an ancient and ongoing "dialogue" between God and his people about what it means to be the people of God in a variety of times and conditions. As members of the family, we are invited to listen in on this dialogue and to participate.

Casebook vs. cookbook – This "dialogue" suggests that the Bible is not a cookbook with specific "recipes" to produce the same results in any given socio-historical context. The Bible is more a casebook filled with case studies of how God and his people have related to each other. Principles can be drawn from these case studies for the present (1Cor.10:6,11)

Reading—Regular time spent in reading reliable, clear translations of the Bible acquaints us with this ongoing dialogue, and provokes us to analyze the case studies and apply the principles in our own lives.

Doing—Understanding the Bible is only the first part of Bible study. In Matthew 7:21-27, Jesus reminds us that intellectual knowledge without obedience is totally insufficient.

Fellowship

While there have been cases of isolated Christians surviving without the benefit of fellowship, it is clearly the exception and not the rule. The Scriptures, the whole history of God's covenant people, know nothing of a privatized faith, lived apart from and with no regard for the rest of the "family." This fellowship is both a giving and receiving activity and can take at least two different and complementary tacks.

Small groups—Fellowship really indicates relationship and this suggests a small group in which the participants encourage each other, support each other, and are accountable to each other. Ideally this group should number between 4 and 12 persons.

Worship and celebration—These are also aspects of fellowship and this is often made more intense and satisfying in the context of a larger group or congregation, in which large numbers of Christians blend their gifts and talents in praise to the Father.

Service

Nobody is simply saved. We are all saved from something and for something. Each person born into the kingdom of God is given one or more gifts (1 Cor.12:7) and these gifts are given for a purpose, for mission and service. It is imperative that each Christian discovers and activates his or her gifts.

Area of service—The arena for the operation of these gifts may be inside the church or outside, but never apart from the church. That is, they may be gifts that are appropriate for worship and service to other Christians (e.g. prophecy or pastoring), or they may be gifts that are needed for the extension of the kingdom of God (e.g. apostleship or missions).

Your role as encourager—As young Christians begin to become involved in prayer, Bible study, fellowship and service, their gifts will become apparent. It is your responsibility to affirm their gifts and encourage them to seek God's guidance in using them in the mission he has given them.

1. You think about your own Christian journey, ask yourself who discipled you and encouraged you to grow as a Christian. How was it done? What was most helpful? What do you wish someone had done for you or with you to assist you on your way to Christian maturity?

2. Find a mature Christian from a culture very different from yours. Ask this person to define "spiritual maturity" and tell you how it is achieved. Write out this response and compare/contrast it with your own.

3. If your faith maturity is deemed appropriate, ask your pastor for the opportunity to disciple a new member under his or her guidance.

22

Staying Fit as a Witness for Christ

A good artisan or mechanic uses the best available tools to produce good results. He actually budgets for new tools, knowing that some will wear out, and newer and improved tools might be available in the future. This is no less true for a missionary. You may have to travel lightly, but don't forget your tools. This chapter introduces you to some of them.

Methods of Studying the Bible

Let's think first about different ways we can read and study the Bible.

Doctrinal Bible Study

This is a topically oriented method of studying the Bible. It focuses on specific teachings and seeks to understand them in the context of the ongoing dialogue that is found in the Scriptures.

A few cautions: The selection of topics is determined by the teacher or the student, not by the Bible. Their theological, denominational, educational, economic, political and cultural background may determine what is studied and what is left out. To be balanced, this method is best done in community, not alone. Also, be aware of the "proof-text" method of Bible study that lifts specific verses or portions out of context. A Bible text must not be made to say something that its context does not support.

Socio-Historical Bible Study

This method of studying the Bible seeks to understand the original socio-historical context of a book or passage and what the text meant to the original listeners. As we listen to the ongoing dialogue in the Bible we learn essential principles for today.

Eschatological Bible Study

This method looks at Scripture through the lens of the cosmic controversy between Christ and Satan in the light of the final judgment and last day events. This method is more appropriate for some parts of the Bible (Ezekiel, Daniel, Revelation) than others.

Devotional Bible Study

This common method asks, "What is God saying to me now? It seeks personal insights from the various case-studies and then applies that message. At its best, this method builds on the other methods.

Relational Bible study

This method is specifically concerned with application. It is best used in a small group setting where people can hold each other accountable. It specifically asks, "How do I (we) apply what I (we) have learned today?"

Reading in the Congregation

The Bible was originally written to be read aloud. The text in Revelation 1:3: "Blessed is the one who reads the words of this prophecy, and blessed are those who hear it and take to heart what is written in it" refers to a public reading in the congregation. In Revelation 22:17,18 a blessing is pronounced on those who "hear" the words of the book. Ask yourself how people might study the Bible without printed copies? How might people study the Bible in a pre-literate society? How might people study the Bible in societies where translations have not yet been made?

Plays and Drama

During the Middle Ages, in pre-literate Europe, morality plays and charades were often used to teach the Scriptures. How might this be adapted today? Imagine what might happen if a group of people were to act out parables of Jesus or healing actions on his part or the story of Zacchaeus the tax collector?

Connecting with the Bible Story

Tom McAlpine (MARC) suggests that you should answer three questions as you search the Scriptures:

- What similarities exist between their experience in biblical times and our experience now? (This question leads to contextualization.)

- What light does their experience cast upon our experience? (This leads to prayerful reflection.)
- What should we do about these insights both as a group and person- ally? (This leads to actualization.)

The last question forms a bridge to new plans for personal and group action, which helps ensure that the principles of Scripture are lived out obediently and practically.

When you come together for Bible study make sure that there is accountability for following through on the principles learned. One author recommends the following steps of studying the Bible, implementing the insights gained and sharing the resulting experiences of seeing God at work in ones life:

- *Invite*: As you open the Word of God remind yourselves that the risen Lord is with us.
- *Read*
- *View with wonder*: We pick out words or short phrases, read them aloud prayerfully and repeat them three times.
- *Listen*: We keep silent for several minutes and allow God to speak to us.
- *Share*: Respond to the question, "Which word has touched us person- ally?" We do not discuss any contribution, even though some may not share personally but comment instead.
- *Plan for action*: Now we discuss any task which our group is called to do in our neighborhood or parish.
- *Pray*
- *Share:* In addition you will share with the group next time what God has done in response to obediently putting the truth learned into action. This step should lead to praise and celebration.

Why Are There Different Translations?

There are a number of excellent books available on the merits and prob- lems of various translations and paraphrases of the Bible. We will give here a short summary and evaluation of the main kinds of translations available. Bible translations can be classified in several different ways:

- *Committee translations* avoid personal biases. Translations done by *individuals* often have more flair and passion than a committee will tolerate. For example, compare Goodspeed's New Testament with the Revised Standard Version.
- *Literal translations* seek to translate word by word. They appear to be more conservative, more amenable to a concordance.

- *Dynamic translations* seek to understand the larger meaning of a passage and translate that meaning into a dynamic equivalent in the contemporary language of a people.
- *Paraphrases* take the thoughts of the Bible and express them in modern idiom without trying to be a translation. These types of Bibles are usually easy to read, but they are free in their interpretation and thus susceptible to the bias of the paraphraser.

Neither approach is better than the other. Used together, they shed light on each other and provide greater insight to the serious student. A basic principle that is consistent with historical Christianity is that people should read the Bible in a translation that uses the latest and best in biblical scholarship and is closest to their own mother tongue.

The New Testament was originally written in *Koine Greek*. This particular form of Greek was the result of the gathering of an army by Alexander the Great from all the provinces of the Hellenist world, with all their dialects. As these dialects merged into a common (*koine*) language, this language was spread by this army from Europe to the Indus Valley. It became the common language of all the Greek-speaking world. Far from being a classical language or a "spiritual" language, it was the street language of that age. Ask yourself what translations approximate this form best in your host language?

Bible Study Helps

There are a number of different Bibles and study aids on the market today that provide greater ease and reliability in Bible study. Here are a few of them.

Concordances. There are a number of good concordances on the market, for the KJV, RSV and NIV Bibles. Strong's Concordance provides the original word in Hebrew or Greek and prevents the student from thinking that one Hebrew or Greek word lies behind a single English word.

Computerized Bibles and helps. If you are using a computer there are a number of computerized Bibles with concordances, background notes, and other helps that give you great freedom of study and analysis.

Bible lessons. There are a variety of printed Bible lessons and videotaped series. While these may be very helpful in North America, they have limited use in other cultures and among non-English speaking peoples. Great care should be taken if these are used at all to use lessons that are created by persons within the host culture or persons close to that culture.

The Jesus Film. Based on the gospel of Luke, it is a faithful adaptation of the gospel. It has been dubbed into hundreds of languages and used to present the gospel to millions around the world in their own language.

Resources for Further Study

Dudley, R. and V. B. Gillespie. (1992). *Valuegenesis: Faith in the Balance.* Riverside, CA: La Sierra University Press.

Koyama, K. (1974). *Waterbuffalo Theology.* Maryknoll, NY: Orbis.

Kraft, C. H. (1999). Three Encounters in Christian Witness. In R. D. Winter & S. C. Hawthorne, eds. *Perspectives* (3rd ed., pp. 408-413).

Krass, A. C. (1978) *Five Lanterns at Sundown.* Grand Rapids, MI: Eerdmans.

Little, P. (1988). *How to Give Away Your Faith.* Downers Grove, IL: IVP.

Mallouhi, C. (1994). *Mini-skirts, Mothers & Muslims: Modelling Spiritual Values in Muslim Culture.* Cumbria, UK: Spear Publications.

Mayers, M. K. (1987). *Christianity Confronts Culture: A Strategy for Crosscultural Evangelism.* Grand Rapids, MI: Zondervan.

McAlpine, T. H. (1995). *By Word, Work, and Wonder: Cases in Holistic Mission.* Monrovia, CA: MARC.

Newbigin, L. (1986). *Foolishness to the Greeks.* Grand Rapids, MI: Eerdmans.

Parshall, P. (1999). God's Messenger. In R. D. Winter & S. C. Hawthorne, eds. *Perspectives* (3rd ed., pp. 456-459).

Pippert, Rebecca M. (1999). *Out of the Saltshaker.* Downers Grove, IL: IVP.

Richardson, D. (1974). *Peace Child.* Glendale, CA: Regal. The powerful story of a redemptive analogy to communicate the plan of salvation.

Sahlin, M. (1990). *Sharing Our Faith with Our Friends without Losing Either.* Hagerstown, MD: Review and Herald.

Samaan, P. G. *Christ's Way of Reaching People.* Hagerstown, MD: Review and Herald, 1990.

Steffen, T. A. (1999). Why Communicate the Gospel through Stories? In R. D. Winter & S. C. Hawthorne, eds. *Perspectives* (3rd ed., pp. 404-407).

White, Ellen G. *The Ministry of Healing.* Mountain View, CA: Pacific Press, 1942. One of the most powerful presentations of Christ's mission and ministry.

The Jesus Film. Possibly the most translated film in the history of humanity, this film, based on the gospel of Luke, is a powerful cross-cultural resource to present the gospel to millions around the world in their own language. Contact the Jesus Film Project at 1-800/432-1997 for further information.

How to Be Prepared

23

How to Do an Area Study

You are about to embark on a journey to a new land where you will be surrounded by a new culture. When you arrive you should expect to sometimes be confused by what is going on around you. Cultures differ in degrees of "strangeness" to you. But there are a number of steps you can take that will prepare you for this journey.

Take a trip to your closest library. If you live near a college or university, take advantage of their library. If your community library is small, check out the local high school library. At the library, do not waste time wandering about. Go directly to the Reference Librarian and explain what you need. Generally there are many resources that can be consulted. For an up-to-date bibliography contact the Institute of World Mission or e-mail the Institute at iwm@andrews.edu to request a bibliography for area studies.

Gathering Your Information

The following pages list some of the questions and items you will want to explore. As you gather the appropriate data you may want to use some logical categories to sort the information.

The Land
- I am going to the country of
- On the continent of
- The climate is
- Some natural resources are
- Its major trade is in: imports/exports/currency

Health and Living Conditions
- Major health risks in the country are
- Availability of hospitals and medical services
- Some local dietary practices
- Eating and drinking precautions
- The national holidays

The Population
- Size of population
- Demographics
    - ____ % of the population is under 18 years old
    - ____ % of the population are women
    - ____ % of the population is urban (lives in cities)
- The national languages are
- The language of the people group I will be working with is:
- Obvious people groups are
- Hidden people groups (e.g. immigrants) are
- General education level
    - For men
    - For women
- Education is available to
- Barriers to education

Transportation
- Common methods of transportation within the country
- Weekly flights in and out of the country

How Is Society Organized?
- Social groups
- Castes
- Tribes
- Clubs
- Relations between sexes
- Leadership determined and recognized by

Common Customs I Should Know upon Arrival
- Forms of greetings
- Forms of farewell
- How to say "no" and "yes"
- Serious "no-no's" or taboos

Useful Expressions
- Hello!
- Good bye!
- Please & thank you
- How are you?

- My name is
- How do you say...?
- Where is the toilet?
- How do I get to...?

Food
- What is commonly eaten? And when?
- How do people eat?
- What specific areas will I have difficulty with? Why?
- Is eating merely a utilitarian affair or a highly social matter?

History
- Where do the people come from and why?
- Their myths of origin
- Their traditional friends and enemies
- Was this country ever a colony? Of which nation?
- Date and circumstances of independence
- Membership in international, political or trade organizations
- Involvement in recent conflicts and/or their resolution

Political Developments
- Their political structure? How was it developed?
- What are the major parties? What are their differences?

Change
- How does change take place here?
- What things do not seem to change?

Religion, Religious Forms, Festivals and Symbols
- Local religions of this area are: traditional, imported, or blended
- Level of Christian missionary activity
- How do the people worship and why?
- What are the major festivals?
- How is spirituality defined or understood?

What Is the History of Christianity in This Country?
- When it was introduced and by whom?
- How it was accepted? By whom? Why?
- If it has been commonly rejected, why?
- The most successful Christian churches or groups here, and why?
- Forms of indigenous Christianity and their history

The Adventist Church in This Country

- What is the history of the Adventist Church in this country?
- When was it introduced and by whom?
- Who has generally accepted or rejected it and why?
- Ways the church has been most successful?
- How does the local Adventist church relate to the world church? Why?

(For information regarding SDA work in a specific country, do not forget to consult the valuable collections of the Adventist Heritage centers; for statistical information check this website: www.adventist.org/ast.)

Resources for Area Studies

The Internet has revolutionized how we locate information. Nevertheless any good university or college library is still a door to a world of print (books, periodicals, pamphlets), media (e.g.: videos), and electronic information. The following list will get you started on finding materials for the country or area where you are going.

Bookmarks to Internet Resources

www.lonelyplanet.com This site allows you to select a destination (country or city) and get very up-to-date information. Also: great facts at a glance feature.

www.iagora.com/pages/html/tools/embassies.html Find the websites for embassies, information offices, and consulates around the world and get the latest visa information with lots of additional stuff. Available in English, France, and Spanish.

travel.state.gov The US State Department site is very informative on all countries of the world: e.g.: customs regulations, contacts and locations of embassies, safety/security, travel warnings, passport and visa information, and international adoption.

www3.travelocity.com/destg This popular travel site gives information on any country, region or city, and lets you book a flight, rent a car or reserve a hotel.

www.mislinks.org MisLinks has become the gateway for mission information of interest to missionaries, mission teachers, researchers, and leaders.

www.odci.gov/cia/publications/factbook/index.html The *World Factbook* contains information on geography, people, government, economy, communication, transportation, and military issues of any country.

www.adventist.org/ast Contains information of the General Conference Archives, the newest SDA Yearbook, and the World Church Statistics database originally developed by our office (Global Research Center) and now maintained by the GC.

www.cdc.gov This is the site of the Centers for Disease Control and Prevention. It provides a listing of disease and health topics for any destination country.

worldmission.adventist.org/ The website of the Institute of World Mission.

You may also want to check out your host country's specific website.

Conventional library resources are still a great way to find a lot of information on many countries. Here are a few types of resources you should consult if you are near a good university or college library.

Encyclopedias and Almanacs
- *Americana*
- *Britannica*
- *Information Please*
- *World Almanac*

World Country Information
- *Cities of the World*
- *Maps on File*
- *Operation World* (2001)
- *Times Atlas of the World*
- *World Christian Encyclopedia*
- *World Factbook*

Popular *series* titles begin with:
- *Area Handbook Series of ...*
- *Cultural Atlas of ...*
- *Peoples of the World ...*
- *People Profiles*
- *Survey of World Cultures*

Specific Country Studies
The library has many works devoted to *specific countries*. Do a subject search: MISSIONS-(Name of the country).

Works Organized by Ethnic Groups (People Groups)
Various organizations have produced materials on the people groups of the world. The most complete one thus far is the following set of papers.
- *People Profiles*, produced by Adopt-a-People Clearinghouse and other groups, such as Frontier Missions Centre of Australia.

Religions, Missions
There are many books on *world faiths* in the religion section of your library. The standard reference is Barrett, D., ed. *World Christian Encyclopedia: A Comparative Study of Churches and Religions in the Modern World, 2d edition, 2001.*

Other works are:
- *Eliade Guide to World Religions*
- *Encyclopedia of Modern Christian Missions*
- *Unreached Peoples Directory*

Adventist Resources
For *Seventh-day Adventist* (SDA) reference materials you may want to consult the following items:
- *SDA Encyclopedia* (two vols.)
- *SDA Yearbook*
- *Statistical Report of the General Conference of SDA's*
- SDA journals published by different fields and institutions
- The Department of World Mission at Andrews University (616/471-6505)
- The Institute of World Mission and the Global Research Center (616/471-2522)

Mission Prayer Guide
Operation World (2001) is an 800-page Christian mission almanac in paperback. You can't afford not to own this rich and inexpensive resource.

Going to the Local Market or Mall

To really connect with a community go to the local market or mall for about two to three hours. Spend the first hour observing, listening to conversations and mapping the area. Attempt to blend in as much as possible and not stand out. Take brief notes unobtrusively and enlarge on them later. The second and third hour ask questions continuing to listen and observe. Finally record your reflections in your field journal.

The Physical Layout
- Where is the site located in relation to the neighborhood and other businesses? Is it easy to get to by car, or by public transportation?
- How much space is devoted to parking? Why?
- How are the stores arranged? Which stores are nearest to the entrances and the exits? What stores are missing? Why?
- What are the window displays like? What age, gender and style are most prominent in the displays? What sounds make up the atmosphere?

The Social Relationships
- What are the different social groupings? How do they interact? Do they mix?
- What kind of relationship can you observe? How is this different than where you have lived?

The Value System
- What values are reflected by the things you observe? What seems to have high or low value? How is this indicated? What social values are reflected in the relationships you see?
- List all the positive and negative aspects you observed.
- What implications could these observations have for your mission? For example, are there possibilities for ministry in this site? How might kingdom values interact with the observable local values?

Observe and Reflect
Use all your senses in your observation. Listen to the voices, noises, sounds, the music, and eavesdrop on conversations. Take in the smells. Taste the foods. Then ask yourself about the meaning of the things you see, hear, smell, and touch. What specific evidences did you see of God at work here? How can you become part of God's presence in this place?

For more complete instructions on how to do an ethnographic study, check our website: worldmission.adventist.org

What to Do in Case of Emergency

Here you are—almost at the end of this book. Ready to go! But before you rush off there's one more important thing we'd like to mention—your safety. No one wants to think about bad things that could happen, but the reality is that we live in an unsafe world. There are natural disasters that can happen anywhere—hurricanes, earthquakes, typhoons. In addition, there can be illness or accidents which are a part of life. In addition crime is a problem everywhere on earth. And finally, there are many places where there is political unrest which may lead to kidnaping, evacuation, and other difficulties.

Though very few missionaries encounter serious problems of this nature, it is nevertheless important that you at least think about them and know what you will do if anything of this nature occurs while you are serving. In fact you want to do everything you can to live aware of your surroundings to possibly prevent problems (see Streetsmarts for Dummies on the next page).

The following guidelines have been prepared by the Institute of World Mission at Andrews University, at the request of the General Conference of Seventh-day Adventists and are the official guidelines for missionaries to follow in emergency situations. Please read them carefully.

Types of Emergencies
When we talk about emergencies we mean the following types of events:
- Hospitalization
- Natural disasters: e.g., Bangladesh, Guam
- Political crises: e.g. Rwanda, Cambodia, Albania
- Evacuation
- Death of a spouse or family member

Streetsmarts for Dummies:
How to Survive on the Streets

If you are not accustomed to urban life, you may feel very uncomfortable in cities. Even cities in your own culture are actually very different from the suburban and rural culture you are accustomed to. Here are some suggestions to help you survive:

- Each city has its own "tempo" or "rhythm." It takes a few days to adjust to the new rhythm, so expect to feel "out of sync" for a time.
- Avoid carrying large purses or clutch purses. Purses should be hung over the body, not the shoulder.
- Separate your credit cards and driver license from your cash. If you are robbed, you only loose the cash.
- Look and act confident. Frightened people are a natural prey.
- Don't stare at people. In general, avoid eye contact on the streets.
- Avoid dark, empty streets.
- Avoid walking around the city at night.
- Women should never get into a cab alone, especially at night.
- Do not give money to beggars. (But always have a few coins for street musicians—they enhance life.)
- If you think you are being followed or feel uncomfortable, step into a store or shop and browse while you gather your bearings. If you feel seriously threatened, ask to use a phone to call the police.
- Subways are generally well lit and safe.
- Remember that most urban people are very normal, friendly and willing to help you. Don't be afraid of everybody.

Things *Everyone* Must Do *before* Anything Happens

• Register with your country's embassy or consulate. This is a *must!*

• Choose a person outside of your country (preferably a family member) who will be the contact person for you and your family. Be sure that your liaison persons at the GC (or your home division), your host division, union and/or mission have the number of this person in case you can't get through to them in time of crisis.

• Know who your line of communication is within your country/mission/ union in case of serious crisis.

• If your institution includes several families, choose one person to be a crisis coordinator who will make key decisions and contact the "outside world" in case of a serious crisis. He should have the homeland contact numbers for all missionaries from your institution/compound so that he can with one phone call get the word out to one person who will then notify everyone of your status. (It would actually be good if your group chose one "homeland crisis coordinator" who has all the contact phone numbers for your entire group. This is a valuable precaution in the event that you can get only one short phone call out.)

• If possible, get to know some people at your country's embassy or consulate and also one or more of the international news agencies. A few friends "in high places" can be very helpful in time of crisis.

• Keep all important documents (passports, ID cards, a few travelers' checks or a letter of credit, some US dollars, local government travel documents, visas, or work permits, as applicable) and important phone numbers—GC hot line 301/ 680-6024, family contact person, local mission, union and/or division—together in a place that is easily accessible in case of a crisis. *Remember: You may be looking for them in a state of panic and under very difficult circumstances.*

• If you have short-term volunteers or independent missionaries working in your area *even for only a few weeks,* be sure the correct embassy, the local crisis coordinator and the organization above you (mission, union, or division) know they are in the country.

• If you are in a sensitive area it would be well to develop some discrete telephone language or a written code for use in a crisis.

Things You Should Do in Case of Serious Illness or Accident Requiring Hospitalization

• Notify your liaison person at the GC or your home division so that they will know firsthand the extent of the problem. (This avoids rumors, speculation and unnecessary worry.)

• If you are responsible for other missionaries (especially student missionaries or other volunteers) be sure and notify the GC department that sent them and their parents, if appropriate (plus their home division if they are not from North America).

• Keep a record of pertinent details in regard to the illness/accident which you can share with family members so that they have a sense of involvement and an understanding of the situation. This is very reassuring to them when they are far away.

Things to Do in the Event of a Crisis Requiring Evacuation or Possible Evacuation

• If communication with the "outside world" is still possible, get advice from the GC and/or the home division personnel assigned to advise you. Remember, they will be in contact with the US State Department (or its equivalent in the other divisions), the embassies of the countries involved, as well as international news agencies and will therefore usually have a reasonably good understanding of the overall seriousness of the situation. *Listen to the advice they give!* When they say "*go*," it is definitely time to *go*! Don't put the local or world church, or the local people or institution in jeopardy by insisting on staying when it is no longer safe–for you or them.

• If communication with the "outside world" is cut off, try to get the most reliable advice available via shortwave broadcasts from out of the country, your country's embassy or consulate, international news persons, and church leaders at the local division and union levels.

• Try to work through your crisis coordinator to avoid confusion.

• During times of crisis (especially political crisis) keep your important documents with you at all time so that you could leave the country at any time and from any place, if it should become necessary.

• During times of crisis keep a small suitcase packed at all times containing absolute essentials so that you could leave at a moment's notice if necessary.

• If possible, have several people in your group keep a log of events leading up to, during, and after the crisis. This type of information may be very valuable at a later time as the event is evaluated locally as well as globally. The log should include phone calls, a chronology of events, times, places, dates, and possibly names. However, due to the sensitive and sometimes dangerous nature of such issues, a person's name in a log kept by a foreigner could put them in serious jeopardy, so in most cases it would be better to refer to people in some kind of code which would not get them into trouble if it were to fall into the wrong hands.

• In your log, include the good things that happen as well as the bad so that when it is all over, those who were helpful can be properly recognized and thanked.

• Gather any information the local people may have of the event. Avoid any contact that may endanger them however. Other missionaries and nationals may be able to get information through their normal contacts better than you can.

• If a witness can make a statement, take it. Get it in writing. If the person cannot sign it or needs to remain anonymous for safety, you write it, describing the informant as "a 50-year old farmer" (or use coded language.) Then you sign it as receiving the testimony of this witness, date it, indicating your location.

• Keep in touch with the local (national) church authorities as well as other missions and churches in the area. Keep a record of their intervention.

• In the event of the disappearance of a missionary, keep a record of where the person lived and worked, the area where he or she was taken, the area where last seen, etc.

What to Do if You Are Abducted

• Remain calm and follow instructions. Do not give your abductors cause to hurt you. Appear cooperative and be polite. Do not argue with or provoke your captors. Listen carefully to their initial demands to make sure you understand what may be demanded of you. The first few moments of a hijacking and kidnaping are the most dangerous to the victim.

• Anticipate denial and disorientation, followed by depression, during the early days of your captivity. You may suffer sleep loss and intestinal disorders as well. These symptoms of anxiety will recede if you are able to reduce stress and adapt to captivity.

• Adapt to dealing with your abductors in a respectful—but not a subservient—manner. Attempt to establish some type of personal relationship with your captors. Win their respect and sympathy. It is not necessary to grovel and plead or demean yourself in any way. Do not lose faith in yourself. Remember, you did nothing wrong! They are at fault, not you. Tell them about your family. Show pictures, if possible.

• Avoid discussion of politics or religion, particularly politics. If your captors wish to talk about their cause, hear them out, but without indicating agreement or disagreement. If asked for an opinion, say that you are not knowledgeable enough to comment.

• Eat, rest and exercise as much as possible. Keep your physical and emotional strength as high as possible. Try to avoid depression, and always keep in mind that law enforcement officials are doing everything possible to end your ordeal. Exercise by stretching in place or by rolling your neck and limbs. Sleep and wash up when you can and eat and drink when you get the chance. Think thoughts of your family, pray, sing to yourself. Do not give up.

Terrorism for Dummies

Since September 11, 2001 terrorism is a household word. It is a global phenomenon and Westerners are particularly vulnerable. So are non-Westerners identified with Western Christian organizations. Since terrorism cannot always be avoided, we need to ask what to do if and when it occurs.

- Maintain a low profile. Do not flaunt your nationality.
- Dress conservatively, seek to blend in locally.
- Always be polite, but not servile.
- Be alert for unusual activity in airports or other public places, but don't seek danger.
- In case of violence, keep close to the floor.
- Avoid congested areas that might be targets.
- Always be sure someone knows where you are and knows your schedule.
- Do not put other people in jeopardy by disregarding evacuation orders.
- Do not talk politics or religion with strangers.
- Commit your life to Jesus and rest in his hands at all times.

• Do not be disturbed by the Stockholm syndrome, i.e. strong positive feelings toward your captors, if it occurs. It is common, normal and may help improve chances for a healthy survival. This phenomenon is named for a bank hostage situation that took place in Sweden. During the course of the ordeal, the victim began to display strong positive feelings for the kidnapper. This is not a problem and, fortunately, not permanent. The malady is very common, particularly in long-term hostage situations. When it occurs, the captors usually make note of it, and experience shows that they are less likely to harm the victims.

• If your captivity is lengthy, it is imperative that you establish regular mental and physical exercise routines. If space is provided, walk daily and do in-place exercises. If you are confined in close quarters, do isometrics or in-place stretching exercises. Keep a mental calendar of what has happened to you. Do problem solving. Make up a story or write a novel in your mind about your experience. Even daydream!

• If you have a *clear* opportunity to escape, take it; but be mindful that your abductors may have laid a trap for you. Statistically, your best chances lie in a negotiated release. The FBI advises that escape should be a "last-resort" activity and is extremely dangerous.

• In the event of a rescue attempt, lay on the floor with your hands on your head; do not move; shout your name; expect to be treated roughly by your rescuers.

• Remember that everything possible is being done to secure your safe release. Keep a positive frame of mind.

Things to Do in the Event of the Death of a Missionary

When there is death by nonviolent causes (No "foul play" involved)
• Get an autopsy if it is deemed appropriate
• Notify the embassy/consulate of the person's home country
• Notify the GC and the family contact person(s)
• Follow the recommended procedures in the GC working policy (Section "M")
• Get the necessary permission to either bury in the local country or send the body back to the home country, depending on the family's wishes.

When there is death by violent causes
• Get an autopsy, if possible, with a complete report on cause of death, the type of wounds, injuries, etc.
• If an autopsy is not possible, get one or two doctors to examine the body. If they are afraid to be named, have institutional leaders or another expatriate (preferably one with a medical background) witness the examination, sign, date and note the place.
• Document, as far as possible, the actual events leading up to the death.
• Follow the same procedure as above.
• Submit a report of the case as you know it that includes:
   ◦ Specific cause of death (bullet wounds, stabbing, strangulation, massive beating around head or vital organs, etc.)
   ◦ Specify the nature of the wounds, (e.g. where the bullet or bullets entered the body, where they left the body, caliber of bullets)
   ◦ Specify how many wounds.
   ◦ Take pictures or draw diagrams to help clarify the nature of the wounds.
• Look for additional evidence at the scene (bullet casings, etc.)
• Ask press representatives who are there to send pictures to Division and/or GC officials as deemed appropriate.
• Have a mission representative (expatriate) hand carry a preliminary medical exam or autopsy out of the country with the photos to the Division or GC.

- Anything that would be needed as forensic evidence (e.g. clothing, etc.) should be hand carried in a plastic bag out of the country to wherever it will be analyzed.
- If possible, notify the international press so that they can tell the story to the world accurately.
- Send a copy of autopsy and/or report and photos to the appropriate embassy in the country of death.

If necessary, enlist the help of embassy officials and/or the government of your home country (including legislative bodies) to help see that justice is carried out. The denominational administration should send copies of the autopsy/medical report, duplicates of the photos and the denomination's "official version" of what happened to them, asking for a full report, if deemed necessary and helpful.

Special Roles at the Time of the Crisis

The role of institutional leadership
- Notify your embassy.
- Notify next highest institutional level or General Conference Office.
- Notify family (unless done by next highest level).
- Notify local (national) church authorities.
- Notify local civic authority (police, etc.).

The role of the crisis communicator
- Notify contact for international network.
- Notify international press representative.

The role of General Conference or appropriate Division office:
- Notify families
- Notify the appropriate denominational channels

Contact your State Department or *Foreign Affairs Office*
- If an investigation is needed you may need to contact the appropriate office in your State Department or Foreign Affairs Office responsible for your area of service.

(Some of this material was adapted from materials by Sean M. McWeeney, Corporate Risk International, and from "Managing Terrorism Risks" by the Ackerman Group.)
An excellent resource on safety issues is Rogers, C., & Sytsma, B. (1999). *World Vision Security Manual: Safety Awareness for Aid Workers.* Geneva, Switzerland: World Vision.

25

Tips for Travel

In this book we have tried to prepare you for your mission adventure. If you have come this far, you may be seriously considering an assignment somewhere. You have done your area studies and know what climate to expect when you arrive and found other helpful tips from travelers that have been there before you. So now it is time to think about your own traveling and packing. To help you we have put together a few tips to consider as you prepare for your trip.

General Suggestions

- Wear a fanny pack instead of a purse to safeguard your traveler's checks, credit cards, passport, etc. Wear it in front, not in back.
- Be sure and have a copy of a) your plane ticket, b) at least the first two pages of your passport, and c) a list of your travelers' check numbers, and keep them in a separate place. This will make replacement much easier if it should become necessary.
- If you need a lock for your suitcase, consider getting a number-coded luggage lock rather than one with tiny keys which get lost easily.

Packing
Almost everybody overpacks, but what is a luxury to one is a necessity to another. This list is not prescriptive, but descriptive. Your list will differ from that of others, but it reflects your personality and peculiarities.
- Roll up your T-shirts, bathing suits and cotton knits, and tuck them around the sides of the suitcase.

- In case your luggage gets lost, always take a carry-on bag (small backpack, day pack or small roller bag) packed with necessary medicine and toiletries (no sharp objects!), camera equipment, valuables, film, something to sleep in, and a change of clothing and underwear.
- Pack folded clothes in large two-gallon plastic self-sealing bags. Take an extra plastic bag to hold dirty items while you are traveling.
- Put luggage tags on both the outside *and* the inside of your suitcase.

Absolute Necessities

- ☐ Toilet gear
- ☐ Small scissors
- ☐ Nail clipper
- ☐ Prescription medicine
- ☐ Very small sewing kit (pick one up at your next hotel)
- ☐ Collection of safety pins
- ☐ Medical kit with clean syringe and needles
- ☐ Travel clock

Strongly Recommended

- ☐ Minimum sets of underwear and socks
- ☐ Swiss Army knife
- ☐ Shortwave radio & batteries
- ☐ Small flashlight
- ☐ 25' of nylon cord for clothes line or tying boxes, etc.
- ☐ 3-4 ziplock bags pint and quart sizes
- ☐ Inflatable pillow and solid eye mask for sleeping on planes
- ☐ Melatonin (for frequent travelers)
- ☐ Set of electrical connectors and small transformer
- ☐ Small Listerine

Luxuries

- ☐ Travel iron (110/220)
- ☐ Extra batteries for radio, clock, flashlight
- ☐ Foam shoeshine kit

Traveling

- Make sure you have your passport and health certificates handy, as well as the necessary visas. You may want to review some of the historical, cultural information on country of destination you have collected.
- Keep a photocopy of the information page of your passport in a separate piece of luggage and leave one copy at home.

- Make sure the proper people know your itinerary: spouse, secretary, superior, etc.
- Prearrange for desired seats. People who do not do this often sit between very large neighbors in the middle seat, fighting for a spot for their elbows to rest.
- When staying over, en route, confirm your next flight as soon as you arrive.
- Arrive one hour before your flight departs at small, US airports
- Arrive 1.5 hours before your flight departs at large U.S. International airports. Arrive 2+ hours before your flight departs at non-U.S. airports

Suitcases
- Generally you are allowed two check-ins and two carry-ons. The check-ins are weighed, the carry-ons usually are not. The size of the plane may dictate the number of carry-ons.
- Avoid expensive, designer luggage and fancy name-tags.
- Hardsides are slightly more difficult to break into, but this is a relative matter. Softsides will stretch for add-ins.
- Wheelies (detachable wheels) must be stowed under the seat, seriously competing with your feet, while roll-ons can be placed in the overhead compartment.
- A purse is not considered a carry-on, except in very small planes.

Dressing for Travel
- Dress comfortably in loose clothing with a jacket or sweater in case the plane becomes cold
- Take your shoes off if you can.
- Consider your destination when you dress for travel, particularly when you cross the equator.
- If you're buying new clothes, buy wrinkle-free or crinkled fabrics.
- Take things that can be worn at least two or three ways.

Money and Valuables
- Take a limited amount of cash (ca. US$100) in ones, fives, tens and twenties.
- Use a credit card for general use. Cash from ATMs generally offer the best rates and lowest charges.
- Take a reasonable amount in travelers' checks, with the list of check numbers in a separate piece of luggage.
- Avoid sidewalk money-changers. We have seen nationals scammed out of hundreds of dollars and not know it until much too late
- Be careful. Pickpockets abound!

Other Considerations

Safety Factors
- Never open your hotel door to strangers or hotel employees you have not requested for service.
- Avoid walking alone in dark cities.
- Avoid driving after sundown.
- Be thankful for airport security people. Don't complain.

Computers, etc.
Computers are very common travel gear today, but require some attention:
- Be particularly alert for computer thieves, especially at the security check points.
- Keep your battery loaded so you can run the computer if requested at the security check.
- Make sure you have loaded on the best games for lonely nights in hotel rooms.
- Printers are very helpful, but not absolutely necessary. Some of us have been known to fax our notes to the hotel office for printed copies.
- Remember that if anything can go wrong with your computer it will probably happen while you are traveling.

International Callback Cards
- International telecommunications changes so quickly that almost anything noted here will be obsolete within ½ hour. If they survive, international callback services are far less expensive than AT&T or MCI.

Coming Home

I remember coming home from my first trip to Russia. What a life-changing experience it had been! I had been in an unbelievable country: beautiful, poor, and confused. I was confused too. I had strange stories to tell. I had met amazing people and immense needs. I had gained new perspectives. There, one dollar could pay for one month's rent. Ten dollars could pay an engineer's monthly wages. Now I felt guilty to indulge in an ice cream cone for a dollar. As I observed the seemingly careless way in which we spend our dollars I also felt angry.

This experience is common for those who return from mission service. The longer you lived abroad and the better you have adjusted to your host culture the more acute you may feel the symptoms of reverse culture shock when you return home. Once home you will have opportunities to share your unique story. How to do that best is part of our topic in this section. Finally, in this chapter we help you think about life after your term of service.

Think about It

- Have you thought about what will happen when you return home from your mission assignment?
- Have you heard other missionaries talk about their experience of coming home?
- What are some of the things you remember?

Re-Entry

So you are on your way home. Soon you will see your loved ones and your friends. You are looking forward to going out to your favorite restaurant. And there are so many experiences to share with them. Just thinking about being home soon fills you with excitement.

Then you are home. Everybody is there to admire you and to listen to your amazing stories at first. But soon the spell is over. People are busy going about their lives. And home is not quite what it was a year or two ago. Life has gone on while you were away and now it is your turn to fit in again. You discover something you did not expect. Something else has changed. It is you!

Reverse Culture Shock

Now that you have experienced a different way of life you suddenly see the contrast with your way of life: the endless rush, the schedules, the materialism, the superficiality and many other things. Things you had taken for granted now seem wrong. What do you do? We all experience a range of emotions during the period of readjustment. What is crucial is not to get stuck in the negative ways of reverse culture shock.

Turtle—A common response is to get frustrated and critical of people who don't seem to care about the world out there or mission. Their "stupid" questions ("Do people in ... really use no toilet paper?") may irritate you. So you may be tempted to just withdraw into your protective shell.

What to do: Remember that there is no way they will be able to share your level of intensity in feeling and experience. You now have an "active under-standing" of another way of life that can't be accessed without the experience of actually living in another culture.

Crusader—You may even try to force your experience on people and to convert them to your viewpoint. You become a crusader for change in your home, your church, your community, your country or your culture.

What to do: Remember that just as you are entitled to live your life the way you chose, you must allow people to make their own choices. We may go through both "stages." Eventually we adjust.

Adjusting to Being Home

One thing that helps is to view your home culture as another "foreign com-munity" that you must approach as you approached your host culture. Your mission experience has pushed the boundaries of your awareness and given you perspectives that you can't get through books or talking to international students at home. To reap the benefits from your mission experience you can do several things.

- *Evaluate your experience.* It is important that you take time to reflect on your experience. What did you learn? How have you changed? What will you do now?
- *Share your story.* One of the greatest benefits of a mission experience is how you can infect your friends and family with a new commitment to missions. Mission multiplies as those who went out tell their stories. What is important is to tell it well.
- *Stay involved in mission.* Your short term mission experience may only be a first step for God to reveal you what he has planned in your life. Be attentive to his leading.

A good resource for dealing with re-entry issues is Storti, C. (2001). *The Art of Coming Home.* Yarmouth, ME: Intercultural Press. For many missionaries the cultural adjustment pains in re-entry are as unsettling as the culture shock first experienced when going out. So don't despair.

Tips to Improve Your Story

Record stories—Keep a journal to help you remember concrete details. The sounds, smells, sights, and conversations will quickly be forgotten without it.

Be ready—People who remember that you went "somewhere" will politely ask, "How was your trip?" Use the occasion to share a one-minute summary of your experience. Use a short story.

Take initiative—Arrange for settings where you can share your experience. Sabbath School, youth meetings, and prayer meetings are good settings to focus on the mission situation you have known.

Speak up—A story told well in a clearly audible voice will be appreciated. Practice diction. Speak as clearly as possible. Don't be guilty of not communicating your excitement just because your voice could not be heard.

Start strong—In your opening, aim at arousing faith with curiosity. Never start with an apology. Try to create anticipation.

Paint verbal pictures—From your opening statement move into the story with vivid details so your audience can visualize the scene (the squeaky chair, the smell of incense, children splashing in a puddle, your own feelings at the time). Select important things. Answer the basic five questions: who, what, where, when, and why. But don't overdo it. Be careful with jargon you picked up while on your trip that your listeners are not familiar with.

Illustrate your story—Dramatize. Act out a conversation, include facial expressions and verbal inflections. Use your slides to illustrate. But be sure to select only quality pictures and to keep them moving fairly quickly and in the sequence of your story. Don't just flash slides on the screen with a running commentary. Using an object may be appropriate when making a point.

Focus on people—Mission is people sending people to reach people. Stories that touch the hearts of listeners are stories of people. Programs, plans, and policies are important, but they are here to serve people. In your stories and slides, focus on people, their faces, thoughts, and emotions.

Convey important lessons—Stories can hold the attention of an audience. But remember you are not there to merely entertain. Every experience of life can serve to illustrate some biblical principle. A brief statement ("You can't outgive God!") or a quotation from scripture ("And the greatest of these is love!") is helpful. But don't belabor the point.

Accentuate the positive—It is important to relate the challenges you have faced in a hopeful spirit. Rather than condemning people for their materialism, challenge them to see the tremendous opportunities to invest in the Lord's work around the world. Don't bemoan your trials. A little humor can help. Your isolated conditions were not the end of the world, but you could see it from there.

Encourage interaction—Give opportunity for questions. Good communication is a two-way street. Listen to the questions. Answer specifically. Don't feel threatened. You have an answer for every question. It may be, "I don't know." Supportive comments, such as "That's a good question," or "Did you catch the significance of Jack's comment?" set a good tone.

Stop on time—Remember that you are back in a culture where time is of supreme importance. Often you will be asked to give a "short report." Don't despair. Just give a Reader's Digest condensed version of your story. Don't go beyond the time limit.

To sum it all up: Don't miss the opportunities to tell your story. God used people with a story like Hudson Taylor or the Adventist pioneer missionary John N. Andrews to spark modern missionary movements.

Based on Ron Blue, "Tell the Story: How to Communicate with Others When You Return." In *Stepping Out: A Guide to Short Term Missions.* Seattle, WA: YWAM Publishing 1992.

Now What!?

Here are a few ways to keep your missionary experience alive:

Share your mission experience with others. Don't try to give everybody who asks you about your mission experience a long detailed report. But be prepared to go beyond the stereotype "I had a great time!" and try to share some brief concrete personal stories that illustrate what you learned.

Ask your pastor for time to briefly share your short-term experience with your church. Sabbath School is an ideal time to share some of your slides, videos and stories with your church. If you have taken time to think through your mission experience you will be able to select those aspects that help your fellow members understand why mission is still important and how we can get involved.

Contribute to the world mission report in your church. Even the weekly mission report can become a way to stay involved. A mission story related by someone who had a first hand taste can be an effective contribution to keep mission alive on the local church level.

Get involved in a GO conference. GO conferences are organized by the Institute of World Mission and the Department of World Mission every two years on the campus of Andrews University. They bring together hundreds of young adults and dozens of Adventist mission agencies, and feature reports, workshops and exciting plenary sessions to focus on the challenges and opportunities of mission.

Support other short-termers preparing to go on a mission assignment. Your experience can be a valuable resource to other missionaries.

Increase your mission offering. This a tangible way you can support the mission of the Adventist church and of worthwhile mission projects. Remember that the general mission offering often provides the funds to keep those projects running that got started by special one time offerings.

Learn foreign languages. One short termer returned from Russia and decided to learn the language in order to communicate more effectively the next time he went to Russia.

Continue to study the people and their situation of your host culture or other cultures that you might serve in the future. Many universities provide studies in international issues. A cross-cultural experience enables to study more empathetically and respond to important issues more appropriately.

Get involved in local community ministries. Our eyes are often more open to mercy ministries when we have lived in poor areas of the world. Christ's mission included the healing of the whole person. The North American urban scene provides many opportunities for Christian social service.

Consider to get involved in longer-term missionary service. Many long-term missionaries started their mission career as a short-term volunteer. Some mission agencies such as ADRA consider short-term experience the doorway to more extensive mission involvement. You may want to take a look at some of the advice in the next section.

Based on Eaton, Chris and Kim Hurst, *Vacation with a Purpose.* Colorado Springs, CO: Navpress, 1991.

1. We are assuming that you have returned from your mission experience. The following seven questions can assist you in evaluating your experience. You may want to do this with a friend who has shared your experience or for yourself.

- What did you like best about your mission experience?
- What was the worst thing that happened to you?
- What is the most significant lesson God taught you during your mission service?
- In which area of your life did you see the greatest changes?
- What one experience sums up what God did through you?
- What is the biggest challenge you face in returning home?
- What thing are you most thankful for to God?

2. As you think about sharing your story, review the tips for better communication in this chapter. Outline a short report you could give with the principles you learned in this chapter in mind.

3. As you think about the future, what are some of the things you plan to do to stay in touch with your experience and continue your involvement in mission?

Promises
for Missionaries

Exodus 4:12 "Now go; I will help you speak and will teach you what to say."

Deuteronomy 31:8 "The Lord himself goes before you and will be with you; he will never leave you nor forsake you. Do not be afraid; do not be discouraged."

Deuteronomy 33:25 "...And your strength will equal your day."

Psalm 27:1 "The Lord is my light and my salvation—whom shall I fear? The Lord is the stronghold of my life—of whom shall I be afraid?"

Psalm 46:10 "Be still, and know that I am God; I will be exalted among the nations, I will be exalted in the earth."

Psalm 56:4 "In God, whose word I praise, in God I will trust; I will not be afraid. What can mortal man do to me?"

Psalm 118:6 "The Lord is with me; I will not be afraid. What can man do to me?"

Proverbs 3:23, 24 "Then you will go on your way in safety, and your foot will not stumble; when you lie down, you will not be afraid; when you lie down, your sleep will be sweet.

Isaiah 12:2 "Surely God is my salvation; I will trust and not be afraid. The Lord, the Lord, is my strength and my song; he has become my salvation."

Isaiah 40:31 "But those who hope in the Lord will renew their strength. They will soar on wings like eagles; they will run and not grow weary, they will walk and not be faint."

Isaiah. 51:5 "The islands will look to me and wait in hope for my arm."

Isaiah 55:4-13 "See, I have made him a witness to the peoples, a leader and commander of the peoples. Surely you will summon nations you know not, and nations that do not know you will hasten to you, because of the Lord your God, the Holy One of Israel, for he has endowed you with splendor.

Seek the Lord while he may be found: call on him while he is near. Let the wicked forsake his way and the evil man his thoughts. Let him turn to the Lord, and he will have mercy on him and to our God, for he will freely pardon. 'For my thoughts are not your thoughts, neither are your ways my ways,' declares the Lord. As the heavens are higher than the earth, so are my ways higher than your ways and my thoughts than your thoughts.

As the rain and the snow come down from heaven, and do not return to it, without watering the earth and making it bud and flourish, so that it yields seed for the sower and bread for the eater, so is my word that goes out from my mouth: It will not return to me empty, but will accomplish what I desire and achieve the purpose for which I sent it.

You will go out in joy and be led forth in peace; the mountains and hills will burst into song before you, and all the trees of the field will clap their hands. Instead of the thornbush will grow the pine tree, and instead of briers the myrtle will grow...."

Jeremiah 1:7, 8 "Do not say, 'I am only a child.' You must go to everyone I send you to and say whatever I command you. Do not be afraid of them. For I am with you and will rescue you."

Matthew 6:33, 34 "But seek first his kingdom and his righteousness, and all these things will be given to you as well. Therefore, do not worry about tomorrow, for tomorrow will worry about itself."

Matthew 24:14 "And this gospel of the kingdom will be preached in the whole world as a testimony to all nations, and then the end will come."

Matthew 28:20 "I am with you always—even to the ends of the earth."

Mark 9:23 "Everything is possible for him who believes."

Mark 16:17, 18 "And these signs will accompany those who believe: In my name they will drive out demons; they will speak in new tongues; they will pick up snakes with their hands; and when they drink deadly poison, it will not hurt them at all; they will place their hands on sick people, and they will get well."

Luke 11:9-10 "So I say to you: Ask and it will be given to you; seek and you will find; knock and the door will be opened to you. For everyone who asks receives; he who seeks finds; and to him who knocks, the door will be opened."

Luke 11:13 "If you then, though you are evil, know how to give good gifts to your children, how much more will your Father in heaven give the Holy Spirit to those who ask him."

Luke 18:27 "What is impossible with men is possible with God."

John 14:12 "I tell you the truth, anyone who has faith in me will do what I have been doing. He will do even greater things than these, because I am going to the Father."

Acts 1:8 "But you will receive power when the Holy Spirit comes on you; and you will be my witnesses in Jerusalem, and in all Judea and Samaria, and to the ends of the earth."

Romans 8:28 "And we know that in all things God works for the good of those who love him...."

Romans 8:35-39 "Who shall separate us from he love of Christ? Shall trouble or hardship or persecution or famine or nakedness or danger or sword?.... No, in all these things we are more than conquerors through him who loved us. For I am convinced that neither death nor life, neither angels nor demons, neither the present nor the future, nor any powers, neither height nor depth, nor anything else in all creation, will be able to separate us from the love of God that is in Christ Jesus our Lord."

1 Corinthians 15:58 "Therefore, my dear brothers, stand firm. Let nothing move you. Always give yourselves fully to the work of the Lord, because you know that your labor in the Lord is not in vain."

2 Corinthians 4:8, 9 "We are hard pressed on every side, but not crushed; perplexed, but not in despair; persecuted, but not abandoned; struck down, but not destroyed."

Philippians 4:13—"I can do everything through him who gives me strength."

Philippians 4:19 "And my God will meet all your needs according to his glorious riches in Christ Jesus."

Hebrews 13:6 "...The Lord is my helper; I will not be afraid. What can man do to me?"

Promise Psalms

Psalm 91

Psalm 46

Psalm 23

Special Promises for Dealing with "Giants" and Other Obstacles

Isaiah 45:2 "I will go before you and will level the mountains; I will break down gates of bronze and cut through bars of iron."

Joshua 23:5 "the Lord your God himself will drive them out of your way. He will push them out before you, and you will take possession of their land, as the Lord your God promised you."

Joshua 13:6 "I myself will drive them out....."

Joshua 17:18 "...though [they] have iron chariots and though they are strong, you can drive them out."

Exodus 23:27-33 "I will send ...ahead of you and...make your enemies turn their backs and run. I will send the hornets ahead of you to drive [them] out of your way....until you...take possession of the land."

Deuteronomy 1:29 "Do not be terrified; do not be afraid.... The Lord your God, who is going before you, will fight for you...."

Deuteronomy 3:22 "Do not be afraid... the Lord your God himself will fight for you."

Miscellaneous Mission Thoughts

"We are asked to do an impossible task, but we work with Him who can do the impossible."

J. Hudson Taylor

"How often do we attempt to work for God to the limit of our incompetency rather than to the limit of God's omnipotency."

J. Hudson Taylor

"All God's giants have been weak men (and women) who did great things for God because they reckoned on God being with them."

J. Hudson Taylor

"God's best gifts are not in things but in opportunities."

Unknown

"We have all eternity to tell of victories won for Christ, but we have only a few hours before sunset to win them."

Unknown

"All that He takes, I will give.
All that He gives, I will take."

Unknown